You Are
Clairvoyant

YOU ARE CLAIRVOYANT

SIMPLE WAYS TO DEVELOP YOUR PSYCHIC GIFTS

BELINDAGRACE

Llewellyn Publications
Woodbury, Minnesota

First North American Edition
First Printing, 2011

First published in 2007 by Rockpool Publishing

Cover design by Liz Seymour, Seymour Designs
Cover astro image © DigitalVision
Editing by Laura Graves

Llewellyn is a registered trademark of Llewellyn Worldwide Ltd.

Library of Congress Cataloging-in-Publication Data
   You are clairvoyant : simple ways to develop your psychic gifts
BelindaGrace. — 1st ed.
      p. cm.
   ISBN 978-0-7387-2723-3
1. Clairvoyance. 2. Psychic ability. 3. Clairvoyants. 4. Spiritual
exercises. I. Title.
   BF1325.B45 2011
   133.8'4—dc22
                                        2011004687

Llewellyn Worldwide Ltd. does not participate in, endorse, or have any authority or responsibility concerning private business transactions between our authors and the public.
   All mail addressed to the author is forwarded, but the publisher cannot, unless specifically instructed by the author, give out an address or phone number.
   Any Internet references contained in this work are current at publication time, but the publisher cannot guarantee that a specific location will continue to be maintained. Please refer to the publisher's website for links to authors' websites and other sources.

Llewellyn Publications
A Division of Llewellyn Worldwide Ltd.
2143 Wooddale Drive
Woodbury, MN 55125-2989
www.llewellyn.com

Printed in the United States of America

ACKNOWLEDGMENTS

There are so many people I would like to thank, all of whom in their own way helped me to bring this book to life.

Many thanks go to my mother and father, who are always a source of encouragement. To all my dear and wonderful friends, I am so grateful for all of your encouragement and support.

Very special thanks go to my publisher Lisa for your incredible enthusiasm and open-heartedness. You are an inspiring lady. Thanks also to my editor Gabiann for your patient guidance, to Liz for working magic on the cover design, and of course, my Spirit Guides and Angels who have helped and guided me in ways that are too numerous to describe.

My heartfelt gratitude goes out to all of you.
BelindaGrace

CONTENTS

EXERCISES

INTRODUCTION

Being clairvoyant or intuitive is not a magical skill selectively bestowed on some people. It is an innate ability everyone can learn to develop, no matter what background or belief system they come from.

Clairvoyant intuition is no more difficult to learn than a new language or operating a computer, but like anything "new" there is a learning curve, so it is necessary to apply yourself and practice. Nothing in this world is achieved without the will to make it happen. I like to call this your Intention.

Clairvoyance is an inner wisdom and connection that has been with you all along, just waiting to be switched back on again. If you have the intention then your clairvoyant abilities will be *reactivated*.

Each person has their own developmental pace. Sure, the Universe will give you plenty of nudges, but it never gives you more than you can handle, so your own clairvoyant skills will open up at exactly the right time for you.

This book is designed to help you develop these skills through simple, effective exercises. Each technique is presented in a logical sequence and practicing each of the techniques will help you become more proficient in all the others.

There is no right or wrong way to experience your developing abilities. Use this book as a guide and my experiences as a reference to help you gauge your own progress, but embrace and learn from your own feelings, as you are the best judge of what feels right or otherwise for you.

I once met a very powerful clairvoyant from America. She told me that in the first year of working with her newly developed awareness, she allowed herself to get carried away with the supposed power of it all. She prayed and prayed to her God to let her see *everything*. One day she woke up and her whole world had changed—she could hear what people were thinking and she could see images around them of the memories of the pleasant and unpleasant things that they had done. She could see who was cheating on their partner, who was stealing money from their employer, who was feeling suicidal and all the other things that are often hidden behind our outer layers of civility.

This experience nearly sent her insane; and just as she had prayed for this ability, she beseeched her God to make it stop. She didn't want to know everything about everyone anymore. Once this deluge stopped, she thanked her Angels and Spirit Guides for the abilities she had been given and resolved to be content with those. So be grateful for your small breakthroughs as they come and be patient; your intuitive development happens at a certain pace for a very good reason.

In the following pages you will hear a little about my own story and how I came to call myself a Clairvoyant Healer. This is a term or title that I love, but most people only focus on the "clairvoyant" and miss the "healer" part. The latter part is of course the most important, because it means that I am using the clairvoyant skills that I have developed over the years to help people feel better.

They come in confused and depressed and leave feeling uplifted and empowered in some way. Predicting the future is not a big part of my practice. Occasionally the Angels will have something to say to a client about their future which is very precise, but generally they advise that there is no such thing as "the future," there is no set plan or arrangement to depend upon. They want us to understand that there are numerous probable realities which can emerge, depending on the choices that you make and how happy you are within yourself in that moment.

What we create in our tomorrows stems from whom and what we are today, so being more aware and connected to your Divine Guidance in the present moment is very helpful. It is important to remember that as a clairvoyant I am simply a Channel—for energy, *Light*, and information. This book is not about my beliefs or opinions; it is about all the things that my Angels and Spirit Guides have taught me throughout my years of practice. What you are about to read is what they have told me to "do" and the information they have spoken through me numerous times in response to my own questions and those of my clients and students.

I am often amazed myself when I hear some of the things I am saying, because I know that they are not a direct product of my own knowledge, thought process, or experience. In fact, they are the opposite, they are the product of not thinking, and just letting the information come through me.

My journey to where I am now has been a long one, with many twists and turns. In this book, I aim to share with you some of the wonderful things that I have been taught along the way by my Spirit Guides, Angels, and other non-physical friends; and perhaps enable you to see your way a little more clearly and avoid some of the detours I encountered. With clairvoyant development, there is no ultimate destination, so enjoying the journey is a must.

Blessings,
BelindaGrace

CHAPTER ONE

How Did I Get Here?

"Have you always been clairvoyant?" "When did you first realise you were clairvoyant?" "How did you become a Clairvoyant Healer?"

These are the most common questions people ask me when they find out what I do for a "living." All very reasonable questions given that most people don't meet a Clairvoyant Healer every day and it is an area shrouded in a bit of mystery. But the other reason I believe people are so interested in the answers to these questions, is that everyone is naturally intuitive and clairvoyant, and it excites them to find out how they might develop these skills. They recognise something of themselves in me and what I do.

I often liken clairvoyance to an artistic skill. Anyone can paint, draw, or learn a musical instrument if they really apply themselves. Even if you are musical or artistic by nature, you still have to take the time and make the effort to refine and develop your raw skills in a meaningful way. You want to be able to be creative and productive "on demand," and becoming well practiced in your techniques will help you with that.

Being clairvoyant is the same. It is an innate skill we are all born with, there are no exceptions. Some people will have more of a flair for certain techniques than others, and some of you may have to practice more or persevere until you find the instrument or technique that works best for you. But with practice and a positive attitude, your clairvoyant and intuitive skills will reawaken in you once more.

When I was a child and a teenager, any information about the so-called supernatural or metaphysical fascinated me. I occasionally had dreams that would show me, in a general or allegorical way, events that would then happen a few days later. I sometimes felt that I could see or hear "ghosts," and I used to astral travel in my sleep so frequently and so clearly that I would sometimes wake with a jolt, feeling air-sick from the up-and-down motions I had been making in the skies.

One night, when I was around ten years old, I woke up to see my grandmother floating in the bedroom at the end of my bed. I saw her long, flowing, grey hair and her nightdress, but I was not afraid, even though I knew she lived thousands of miles away in Switzerland! Having just awoken from a deep sleep, I blinked and looked again, but she was still there. She waved, but she seemed to be looking off somewhere into the distance and after waving for a while, she simply drifted away through the wall.

The following morning, a telephone call from Switzerland came to advise my mother that her mother had passed away.

Twenty years later another interesting event on my mother's farm prompted a discussion about "spirits" and what happens to people after they die. It was then that I told my mum about what I had seen the night my grandmother had died. Mum was amazed because it had been reported to her that minutes before my grandmother drew her last breath, she had sat up in bed as best she could and waved to something or someone seemingly off in the distance.

By now, you're probably thinking, "Well she was obviously born with this ability; I can't do that kind of thing." But I never thought of myself as clairvoyant or as having some sort of gift. Take a few minutes to think back on your own childhood and you will probably find that you too had some interesting experiences or dreams that were usually explained away by your parents as being just your imagination.

Many of us had invisible friends and believed in ghosts or spirits, or just *knew* things in advance when we were children. These experiences are a result of our natural intuitive faculty, which sadly gets shut down in most children as they grow up, because we live in a world that does not know how to help us explore and expand on these natural gifts.

Back then, these were seemingly random events and certainly didn't happen at my beck and call. They happened *to* me and I often could not predict or even make sense of them. As my teens turned into my twenties, I became much more concerned with the "real world"; most of these kinds of experiences became a thing of the past, with one notable exception.

In 1985 I was travelling in California with my boyfriend. We had very little money and decided to try hitchhiking from Los Angeles to San Francisco to avoid the cost of bus fare. We had intended to only accept rides that would take us along the coastal roads, but one very kind fellow said he would take us all the way to Santa Barbara if we didn't mind an inland diversion through the desert. We agreed, and settled back to enjoy our free and scenic ride.

After some time of driving up a long, gentle slope in the vast terrain, we came up and over the crest, revealing a large shallow valley spreading out before us for miles. My heart jumped, because even though I had never been there before physically in this lifetime, I recognised this place as somewhere I had flown over numerous times in my astral travels! It was an amazing experience to be there again, this time on the ground.

Once again, even though that experience excited and shook me up somewhat, there was nothing I could really "do" with it, I just accepted it and moved on.

After graduating from high school and studying fashion design for three years, I headed out to travel the world. My intuitive connections had already shut down; ignored as I concentrated on the demands of everyday life. I remained in London for three years; enjoying the life of the consummate party girl and took to drinking, smoking, and the work hard/play hard lifestyle with gusto.

If anyone had said to me that I would be a Clairvoyant Healer with a thriving practice one day, I would have considered them crazy.

In London I worked as a sales rep for a great company in Covent Garden, full of young people, many from other countries just like me. The friends I made there are people I treasure and stay in contact with to this day.

My life was all about business, money, travel, and most of all, having fun. But as my social life flourished, my health deteriorated. What I didn't know then was that the deterioration of my health and the bucket loads of antibiotics prescribed to me by doctors would lead me to the place that I am at now.

As much as I loved England, the time came for me to return to Australia and the industry I was convinced I was cut out for—fashion.

I entered the fashion industry, rising through the ranks as state sales manager, national sales manager, and finally landing a great job as a buyer for a national ladies wear chain. A good salary, a company car and business class overseas travel were all part of the job. I should have been happy, but the opposite was true, I was very depressed emotionally and my immune system, already weakened by my previous London lifestyle, became weaker. My bouts of chronic tonsillitis became worse and the medications stronger.

My health was spiralling downward at an alarming rate and I didn't know what to do; antibiotics became penicillin, small doses became large, and still no real improvement was forthcoming.

My emotional health was also teetering. I can remember being so depressed in those last months in the fashion world that I could hardly get out of bed. Crying as I showered and dressed to go to work became the norm.

What I didn't understand then was that I was so out of harmony with my own truth, that I was making myself miserable and ill. I thought there was something wrong with me at a psychological level. Then, as it always has, the Universe handed me a lifeline, and following my flatmate's advice, I went to see an alternative health practitioner who helped change the course of my life.

After nearly two years of homoeopathic remedies, herbal mixtures, and kinesiology treatments, I felt much better and was able to realise that the lifestyle and career path I had chosen weren't what I needed or really wanted. I announced that I wanted to change my life and do something in the alternative health field. My practitioner suggested that I study homoeopathy, which seemed to trigger a prophetic dream that very same night, and a certainty in me about this new direction.

Simply put, my dream was one of me standing on a beautiful beach at dawn. There was a lovely, old timber door floating out over the horizon, and as the sun came up, the door slowly opened, bathing me in the warm and glowing light. A beautiful dream to be sure, but it wasn't just the content of the dream that inspired me, it was the *feelings* I had during it and after I woke up. I felt so calm and happy, and was certain I had been led to my new path.

Later that day, I enrolled in a natural therapies college and never looked back.

Although I do not practice homoeopathy professionally any more, it was what led me to the Clairvoyant Healing work I do now, as I met people who introduced me to other courses of study in the healing realm. Eventually, I was accepted into a small class taught privately in a woman's home on Sydney's lower North Shore. There were about ten of us in this group and we worked together for two years. Our teacher taught us the basics of Channelling, seeing auras or energy fields, and how to feel and sense the chakras.

Finally the day came when I had graduated from college with my Diploma of Homoeopathy and two years of studying the basics of spiritual healing under my belt. Oddly enough, I still saw myself as a homoeopath, believing that most people would not be interested in the chakra-balancing work, let alone be prepared to pay for it.

After months of struggling with very few homoeopathy clients to help me pay my bills, I decided to let people know I could balance chakras. That was really all I could do. Sometimes I would receive a little information, and I could sense the chakras spinning and see their colours in my mind's eye, but that was it.

What amazed me was the interest that was aroused and the large number of clients who came in for what I regard now as a very simple treatment. My practice was in North Sydney, so most of my clients worked in the local corporate offices, some of them at very high levels. It often happened that if one of my clients was a CEO, GM, or MD, he or she would instruct me not to phone their office—they didn't want other people at work to know that they were visiting someone like me. Despite all the hide and seek, most of my clients were extremely receptive and appreciative; proving this to me on a regular basis by recommending me to others (eventually!) and helping this area of my practice take off.

CHAPTER TWO

The Universe Gives Me
My Big Break

All of this was well and good and I was delighted to have clients and an increasingly stable source of income, but I was stubborn. I had just finished three years of homoeopathy study and was undertaking a fourth postgraduate year while I built up my practice. Not recognising the clues that the Universe was giving me, I continued to believe that I was supposed to be a homoeopath and that the chakra balancing—the area of my practice that was really taking off—would simply remain a useful sideline.

I went to great lengths to market myself as a homoeopath and convert my chakra-balancing clients into homoeopathic clients as well, mostly to no avail. Lost in my idea of "the way things should be" and needing a stronger hint, the Universe decided that it needed to give me a kick in the backside—metaphorically speaking of course!

I received the cosmic boot whilst balancing the chakras of a new female client. This young woman was no more than twenty-five, but there was something a little disturbing or dark about her energy, despite her friendly and open personality.

As I worked upon one of her chakras it was as though someone suddenly switched on a large, full colour screen inside my mind. I could see terrible scenes of soldiers beating and even shooting unarmed civilians. They looked like peasants being persecuted by armed forces and I had the immediate feeling that it was somewhere in South America. Not knowing what to do, I watched for a few seconds in utter amazement. I wondered *"What is going on here?"* and I heard a voice inside my mind explain: *"It's her past life. Tell her about it."*

I have no idea how well I did that day. I did my best to describe everything to her that I could see, hear and feel; this same voice speaking through me to fill in a lot more of the detail.

My client was intrigued and felt that she could relate to much of what had come through in the "story." She had no idea that this was the first time I'd experienced this kind of information download, and while she left feeling lighter than when she had come in, I was left to ponder the meaning of what had just occurred.

As days turned to weeks and my practice continued to expand, the downloading of these movies and the commentary that accompanied them became clearer and more detailed.

I still wrestled with my belief that I was destined to be a homoeopath for a while, realising only much later that homoeopathy, and that all-important diploma, was the path by which I was meant to arrive at this place.

I have an enormous respect for homoeopathy and the dedicated practitioners that work with it. The four years of study gave me a foundation and confidence to deal with clients that I wouldn't have had if I'd studied Clairvoyant Healing alone. To this day, I still visit my own homoeopath here in Sydney for a chat and a remedy, and derive much benefit from it, but it was not meant to be my actual career—it was the thing that prepared me for what was.

As for my interesting "sideline"—well, it completely took over my practice and I finally learned to let go a bit and do what I was told! Now, I know what you are thinking, no matter how hard you tried, this sort of thing would never happen to you, but the truth is it could and does happen to any number of people, and even more so if you are open and receptive to it. Undertaking the techniques in this book is, in part, your message to the Universe that you are ready and willing to listen to whatever it needs to tell you.

Remember, it took me a while to really listen too, but after that initial experience, I decided to *trust* what I was being told and shown—the most important requirement of all when it comes to developing clairvoyant abilities. Instead of negating these experiences, I realised that all the information was coming to me because the client on the table needed to know about it.

Instead of getting in the way, I decided I would be the clearest channel for this information that I could be.

The only confirmation that has ever mattered to me is feedback from the clients themselves. If they had looked at me like I was crazy and told me I was talking a load of rubbish, then the only sensible thing to do would have been to stop. Instead, I found time and again that my clients related so much to what came through me that they often cried, usually hugged me, came back for more, and sent their family and friends in as well.

Since those humble beginnings, I have also developed courses through which I am able to teach and share what I do with small groups of students. It always amazes and delights me when I see how quickly they blossom in things that took me years to learn. Within weeks, many of my students are reading past-life information, communicating with angels, and balancing chakras in a natural and confident way. They are living proof that you can do this work too if you are simply willing to try.

The techniques you are going to learn and use from this book will help you be as clairvoyant as you wish to be in your life, but only if you practice them. I didn't just wake up one day and feel: *Wow, I'm clairvoyant!* I worked at it for years in class and on clients to hone my skills. Every time I received instructions or guidance to do something new, I followed it without question, because I always felt safe, protected, and loved while

I did this work. My clients' positive feedback helped immensely as well.

Every technique described in this book has been taught to me by my Angels and Spirit Guides—my teachers— for the last ten years, and are the same techniques I teach in my classes.

You will learn how to meet your own celestial friends and how to develop your clairvoyant and chan- nelling skills in various ways. Like me, you should let your feelings be your guide, and if you are more com- fortable using some techniques than others, you should persevere with them.

Not everybody wants to do what I do as a profes- sion, but we can all use more information, guidance, and clarity when it comes to navigating the journey of life. The techniques you will learn from this book will help you to become more connected to a higher source of guidance and awareness than available if we only rely on our intellectual knowledge or logical minds.

Many people come to see me because they feel stuck, uninspired, lost, or depressed. They have lost contact with the meaning and purpose of their lives. So these are the tools we give to them in order to help them bring that meaning and purpose back.

There are many different and valid ways to approach and make the most of your life's journey. This book does not claim to hold all the cures for personal and societal ills.

It is a starting point, and I believe a very important one, because it demystifies something that all of us have; a profound and natural intuitive and clairvoyant capacity. I trust that you will enjoy uncovering, rediscovering, and developing your own.

CHAPTER THREE

Why Your Imagination Is Your Most Important Tool

The imagination is your interface and interpreter. It is the bridge between the physical and the non-physical worlds, and if you let it open up new worlds and understanding for you, it will prove to be a great gift.

How many times have you heard someone say: *"Oh, it's just your imagination,"* or *"I was probably just imagining it."*

Statements like these can sometimes imply that the imagination is a second-rate or unreliable function of our minds. For many people, the imagination is not "real"; it is considered to be something untrustworthy or even worse, something to be feared.

These days, many people look to science as the only reliable measure of what is true and real in our world, yet the same scientists who develop their tests, theories, and concepts are using their imaginations to do so. You could say that our imagination is the first step in the creation of anything, whether it is building a computer, designing an item of clothing, or creating a work of art. Before any item can be created in the physical realm, it has to start as an idea. Where would the human race be without imagination?

In the same way that our imagination helps us bring something to life, it also helps us to connect with the levels of life we cannot perceive with our five physical senses. There is much more going on around us than what our eyes can see or our ears can hear.

For instance, dogs can hear a much higher pitch than our human ears can, and certain types of tropical fish can see colours outside the spectrum we consider to be normal. Electricity is not visible, yet much of our world runs on it, and waves of different frequencies create for us the very real experiences of listening to the radio or watching television.

Just as a television or a radio needs an aerial or an antenna to receive this information and the wiring within to translate it into sound or pictures for us, so too do we humans have ways of collecting and translating information from the Universe for ourselves. I call these the *Channel* and the *Inner Screen.*

In the next chapter, I will describe to you how to reactivate those parts of your spiritual anatomy that will enable your antenna to start receiving again. For now, however, I would just like you to contemplate the idea of your imagination as the interpreter that takes newly received data and helps you decipher it.

The music on your radio and the pictures on your television screen are transmitted in certain formats and later translated into others so that your senses can comprehend them. When your Channel receives information from your Divine Guidance, Guardian Angel, the Universe, or whatever you would like to call it, your imagination converts those frequencies into feelings, thoughts, words, or images you can understand.

Your imagination is the bridge, the vital link we all have, between our physical and nonphysical worlds. In order to exercise and strengthen your imagination, and help your vital link to function, there are some simple exercises you can do. You won't need to set aside much time to do these exercises either, as you can do them while performing simple tasks like going for a walk or going to and from work. There is nothing difficult about developing what is already one of your natural assets! It is meant to be easy, interesting, and fun. The most important ingredient is your intention, and if you intend to let the words in this book and the Universe guide you, wonderful results will come your way.

Exercise One

Exercising Your Imagination

When people say they can't visualise things very well, especially something not normally seen, like an angel, I ask them to imagine something more common to their everyday experience. This exercise is designed to help you get used to using your imagination and by doing it, you will reactivate your Inner Screen, the mind's eye which interprets information and guidance into visual pictures

Requirements: A quiet space where you can sit or lie comfortably

Time required: A few minutes

- Close your eyes. Sit quietly for a minute or two and allow yourself to visualise a red sports car with lovely, shiny chrome wheels, a roof that comes down, and white stripes along its sides. You will be able to imagine it even if you have never seen a car exactly like this before.

- Use your own imagination to fill in the gaps—you create it yourself—the whole point of using your imagination in the first place. Your red sports car will be unique to your own imagination, because you have put your own original spin on it.

Variation

Another way you can exercise your Inner Screen is by deciding what clothes you want to wear at a future point in time.

- Close your eyes and imagine what you may wear to work tomorrow, or picture an outfit you could wear to a party on the weekend.

- In your mind, go through your wardrobe and imagine yourself in this or that outfit until one feels right.

- Hold these images for a few moments then let then them fade. Repeat this simple exercise for a few moments each day This is your imagination in action, and this exercise gives you a good example of what clairvoyant sight feels like. It is not like seeing a solid object with the naked eye, but it is just as clear and real.

Once you become accustomed to this practice you can challenge yourself by trying to imagine an Angel, allowing your imagination to create an Angel which is unique to you.

EXERCISE TWO

IMAGINING AN ANGEL

Requirements: A quiet space where you can sit or lie comfortably

Time required: A few minutes

- Close your eyes and sit quietly for a few moments and give yourself permission to imagine an Angel.
- Imagine this Angel however you would like it to be. It won't matter if you have never "seen" an Angel before, as you can determine exactly what your Angel looks like. Maybe your Angel will look like the traditional representation with big white wings and a halo, a small

cherub, or even a ball of pure silver light. However your Angel appears to you is fine; there is no right way or wrong way to imagine an Angel.

- Let the image form gently in your mind. Do not try to grab onto any particular image. Welcome them all as they come and allow them gently to fade away.
- Take pleasure in this simple exercise and let it be fun. Repeat it for a few minutes whenever you like.

Your imagination is a very valuable tool. Use it, exercise it, treasure and respect it because it is your vital link to the beauty and magic of all the non-physical levels of life.

The suppression of our truly creative and original imagination is one of the great tragedies of human life. When someone has a great idea or a child shows artistic talent, it is often disregarded because it has no monetary value. Using your imagination is not the same as being impractical or trying to escape reality, it is one of the tools given to us so that we may expand and evolve as human and spiritual beings; it is the birthplace of all the things we consider to be real.

Now we come to the most important point about your imagination, this wonderful tool we all have that needs to be nurtured and cherished. Your imagination is the *bridge* between this physical reality and all the other realities you long to connect with.

Imagination is synonymous with inspiration; it is the link between the Divine Guidance we all need and the thinking mind that can decide to act upon it. It literally bridges the gap between what is tangible to our senses as human beings and that which is available to us in unlimited quantity as spiritual beings. You will never be truly intuitive or clairvoyant if you do not engage your imagination.

Your Divine Guidance will bring you support and inspiration in a way that is uniquely tailored to your understanding, and your imagination will help to translate it into a form that your mind can relate to and work with.

No two people will ever imagine something in exactly the same way. Spirit Guides can appear to us in unlimited ways. Your Spirit Guides and Angels will look different from anyone else's even when it is an Angel that everyone knows about, such as one of the Archangels. They are not restricted to a physical form and can change their appearance at will.

The human obsession with nailing everything down and the belief that this is the right way so everything else must be wrong is very destructive indeed. In many people's eyes, you would be deemed wrong to imagine an Angel to be anything other than a brightly lit being with wings. Let me tell you now that you wouldn't be wrong because you cannot put limitations on something that is truly without limits.

Use the affirmation for imagination which heads this chapter whenever you need to feel proud of your imagination and your ability to use it constructively in your life. It is a gift that all of us have and all of us need to nurture in order to benefit ourselves and the wider world we touch every day.

CHAPTER FOUR

Getting More Connected— Your Chakras, Channel, and Inner Screen

Remember back in chapter two when the Universe gave me a shove in order to help me see some past-life information for my client? Well it was the daily tune-ups I gave my own chakras, Channel, and Inner Screen that enabled me to receive all that detailed information. Six months prior to that breakthrough, I wasn't seeing or hearing much at the clairvoyant level. Almost every day I did one of the exercises I am going to describe for you. Shortly thereafter, my connection improved, slowly but surely.

I again noticed this improved connection when a lady in her midfifties came to see me. As soon as I put my hands on her navel chakra, I heard the word "hysterectomy" repeated over and over again. Finally I worked up the courage to ask her if she'd had such an operation.

At first, she looked a bit startled but soon opened up about what an awful experience it had been, how there had been complications during and after the operation and infection and continuing soreness in the scar tissue. Her emotional response as well as physical discomfort from the procedure was still very strong even though the operation had been fifteen years earlier.

I went with my feelings and spent most of the treatment time sending the healing light and energy into that part of her body. Months later, she sent me a card to let me know that the discomfort in that area of her body had diminished a great deal after that session, and her hormone balance and moods improved. If I had not been open to receiving her information, the woman would not have had the benefits from this chakra clearing.

Many interesting experiences like this continued to happen, and the more I worked on strengthening and clearing my own spiritual anatomy, the more detailed the information became. Since the day of my "big break through" the expansion hasn't stopped. I continue to do what I call my Spiritual Maintenance and the Universe keeps teaching me more new and wonderful techniques.

The phrase "use it or lose it" doesn't apply only to your physical and mental fitness, it applies to your intuitive fitness as well. Remember, this is just the beginning of your journey—it all gets better from here.

To put it another way, imagine there's a faucet in your home that you haven't used for years and one day, you turn it to let the water flow again. You won't get clear, clean water at first. The pipes may have become rusty; there will be air bubbles and other obstructions. The water will sputter and spurt and be grubby.

Do you give up on it, turn it off, and walk away? No, of course not! You let the water run for a while and use it regularly until it runs normally; the very act of using it is the repair and maintenance required. So it is with your spiritual anatomy. You will be a bit rusty at first, but there is no reason to be disheartened. By doing the following exercises regularly you will get your "water" flowing again, no problem.

Your chakras, Channel, and Inner Screen are the three most important tools that you will work with from now on. As a budding clairvoyant, you'll learn that keeping your chakras healthy and strong is vital. I will give you some techniques for activating your Channel and Inner Screen shortly, but first, let's cover the basics about the chakras so you can understand why they are so important and get you motivated to give them regular care.

CHAKRAS—A BEGINNER'S GUIDE

There are thousands of books about chakras, their history, purpose, and function, but at this stage you only need to know the nutshell version. Some of you may already know more than what is written here—if that's the case, feel free to skip forward to the exercise.

The word *chakra* comes from the ancient language of Sanskrit and means "wheel of light." The chakras are major energy centres within us that support all the functions of our physical and spiritual bodies. Buddhist and Hindu texts have been referring to the importance of balanced and healthy chakras for around five thousand years.

Having a basic understanding of the chakras and their purpose is very helpful in many areas of life. They greatly affect your physical, emotional and spiritual health. We all know how our blood circulates through the body, delivering life-giving oxygen and nutrients to every tissue and cell. We have also come to understand that our circulation aids in the removal of unwanted, toxic, or spent materials from our bodies. When blood circulation is poor, it can affect our health in many different ways.

The chakras and the many channels of energy that connect them, known as *nadis,* work in a very similar way. There are seven main chakras in your body, located individually at the base of your spine, just below your navel, at your solar plexus, at the centre of your chest, over your throat, on your forehead above the bridge of your nose, and on the top (crown) of your head.

There are also chakras on the soles of your feet, in and over every joint in your body, and placed all around you in your aura or energy field. Some ancient Indian texts detail the existence of as many as 88,000 chakras! All these chakras are then connected to each other through the network of nadis to form a vast circulation system for Universal energy, which isn't the kind of energy we'd normally think of like calories or physical energy, but that beautiful, subtle, vital energy normally referred to as prana, qi, or chi.

To an intuitive or clairvoyant, the chakras appear like spheres, circles, or cones of spinning, coloured light. Often when I am working with one of my clients, their chakras will display these characteristics along with many other forms. Frequently I will see their chakras as flowers: sometimes large and flat like gerberas, sometimes like roses, and at other times like the classic lotus flowers described in many ancient spiritual texts.

In a healthy state, the chakras will spin evenly and quickly; each one will glow brightly with the particular colour of the light spectrum at which it vibrates. Altogether, the seven main chakras make up the colours of the rainbow.

A weak, tired, or stressed chakra can feel very sluggish or have a very unbalanced, elliptical spin. On your Inner Screen, you might see the chakra as being dull or dark, rather than the lovely bright colour it should ideally be.

All chakras have very special functions and no one is more important than another. In time, as you learn more about them you will realise that they all have a vital role to play. For the purposes of developing your intuition, the brow chakra (the third eye) is the one most people have heard about and we will be discussing its function in more detail later.

Put simply, the chakra system draws in energy or life force from the Universe and distributes it throughout your body and energy field. The chakras also give out energy and are significant in composing the "vibe" that each of us feel from other people and emanate from ourselves.

Have you ever wondered how it is you can sense another person's happiness or anger without even speaking to them, or why it is you're drawn to certain people and not to others? The condition and activity of each person's chakra system creates a flow of energy around the person that is unique, and whilst the quality of this energy can fluctuate a great deal depending on mood, health, circumstances, and so on, it will always reflect a person's total composition at any given moment.

Each chakra has a special significance and function, and corresponds to certain areas of your physical body, emotions, and stages of life. Here's a basic guide to the seven main chakras.

The Crown Chakra: The thousand-petal lotus, located on the top of your head.

Colours: Violet, gold, white

Body/mind connection: The brain

Elements: All

Senses: That which is beyond our senses

Represents the connection to our purest form of being. A healthy crown chakra takes you toward pure consciousness and unity with the Universal energy. It is the chakra of enlightenment.

The Brow Chakra or Third Eye: The ninety-six-petal lotus, located on the forehead just above the bridge of the nose, extending from the front to the back of the head.

Colours: Indigo, magenta

Body/mind connection: Face, eyes, ears, sinuses, pituitary gland

Elements: All

Senses: All, including intuition and clairvoyance

Represents knowledge and awareness of being. Takes you beyond an active mind and intellect to a deeper understanding of Universal truths. Increases your capacity for visualisation, trust in your intuition and an ability to see beyond the surface meanings of life. Functions as your all-important Inner Screen, acting as a portal for all that you will see. It is the chakra of the Divine Wisdom that is available to all of us, beyond the conscious mind.

Meditating on your brow chakra and on the creation of your Inner Screen will reactivate and strengthen it.

Fluorite is one of the many crystals that is said to increase the powers of your brow chakra and second sight.

The Throat Chakra: The sixteen-petal lotus, located over the throat, extending from the front to the back of the neck.

Colours: Sky blue, bright blue

Body/mind connection: Voice, throat, jaw, neck, arms, and verbal expression

Element: Ether

Sense: Hearing

Represents the way you express yourself. A healthy throat chakra improves self-expression so that you may be truthful and clear. Also aids knowing when to be silent and listen to others or your own inner voice. It is the chakra of communication.

The Heart Chakra: The twelve-petal lotus, located over the lower sternum in the centre of the chest and extending through the chest to the back, between the shoulder blades.

Colours: Emerald green, pink

Body/mind connection: Arms, heart, chest, lungs, skin, thymus gland, circulation

Element: Air

Sense: Touch

Represents the ability to give and receive love freely and unconditionally. When healthy, it enables you to feel compassion for yourself and others, and experience the pure joy of living. It is the chakra of feeling empathy with all other living beings.

The Solar Plexus Chakra: The ten-petal lotus, located on the centre of the midriff, extending to the back.

Colour: Golden yellow

Body/mind connection: Stomach, digestion, nervous system, gut feel, instinct

Element: Fire

Sense: Sight

Represents the way in which you present yourself to the world. Brings a balanced attitude to the spiritual and material needs in your life and promotes acceptance of self. It is the "I am" chakra and is connected to your development as an individual.

The Navel Chakra: The six-petal lotus, located on the lower abdomen, just below the navel and extending to the small of the back.

Colour: Orange

Body/mind connection: Reproductive organs, kidneys, bladder, lymph, body fluids

Element: Water

Sense: Taste

Represents fundamental creativity of and in life. Allows you to be open to the flow of energy between male and female. Enhances a balanced approach to sex, nurturing, emotions, and intimacy. It is the chakra of family, relationships, and belonging.

The Base Chakra: The four-petal lotus, located at the base of the spine, between the legs.

Colour: Rich, crimson red

Body/mind connection: Bones, teeth, nails, blood, muscle, the building of cells

Element: Earth

Sense: Smell

Represents your will to live, survival instincts, and the connection to Mother Earth and Nature. A healthy base chakra keeps you in tune with the natural cycles of life, helps you to thrive and prosper, and keeps you centred and grounded. It is the chakra of our physical form and embracing physical life as part of the human tribe.

Once you have an understanding of how the chakras work, it's important to give them a little tune-up from time to time. Daily is ideal, especially if you are exposed to a lot of people or negativity on a daily basis. A few minutes a day taking care of your chakras will help to keep them and you feeling good, and will definitely make it easier for you to develop your intuition and clairvoyance. So let's get to it!

My Angels taught me that the simplest way to keep your chakras strong, clear, and healthy is to purify them with Light. You can use white light or a rainbow, which-ever you prefer. The chakras resonate to the colours of the rainbow—red, orange, yellow, green, blue, indigo, and violet. White light contains all of these colours, so imagining a rainbow or beam of white light flowing through your body will do the same job. Each chakra will absorb the colour it needs from this spectrum to help strengthen and clear it.

EXERCISE THREE

CHAKRA CLEARING AND BALANCING

Requirements: A quiet place where you can sit or lie comfortably

Time required: 2–15 minutes per day

- Begin by sitting or lying down comfortably and closing your eyes.

- Imagine a beautiful beam of white or rainbow light flowing from the heavens down into the top of your head. Picture it streaming in a strong, continuous flow, moving down through the centre of your body to the base of your spine. Just imagine the rich, healing light flowing through and nurturing all of the seven main chakras.

- Along the way, this light will travel through each of these chakras, entering at the crown chakra on the top of your head and finishing at the base chakra and the base of your spine.

- Breathe deeply and relax so you enjoy this process, it takes very little effort and is really more a matter of just allowing it to happen rather than "doing" it.

- Slowly open your eyes and enjoy the feeling of the energy flowing through your chakras and body as you bring yourself back to the room, re-orientating yourself with your surroundings.

Don't get stressed if you have trouble visualising the beam of light. It's nice to be able to see it, but not necessary in order for the process to work. Your intention is the most important ingredient in all of these processes—as long as your general intention is to let the light flow to and through you for strengthening, balancing, and cleansing your chakras, that is exactly what will happen.

How long and how often you give yourself this little treat is up to you. Spoil yourself and do it every day if you can! Between two and fifteen minutes a day is plenty. You can do it when you wake up as a refreshing way to start your day, before you go to sleep at night to help you relax, or if you commute to work via public transportation then go ahead and do it on the train, ferry, or bus. The cleansing doesn't need to be any more complicated than that.

Once you have cleared your chakras, it is time to concentrate on your Channel. Now, if your chakras are the luminous flowers or energy centres of your bodies' spiritual anatomy, then your Channel is like the great stem or trunk from which the seven main chakras grow. I sometimes like to refer to the Channel as your antenna because it is the instrument that you will activate and use in the receiving of all your Divine Guidance, whether it comes in words, sounds, pictures, or as feelings.

Your Channel is already active to a certain degree, because just like the chakras, your Channel plays a vital role in the distribution of the life force energies in and around your body. In a sense, the Channel is the major nadi, equivalent to the largest artery. It is also known as the *sushumna,* but the word "Channel" is widely understood and will certainly suffice here.

A healthy Channel has the appearance of a strong and colourful beam or tube of light that shines down into your crown chakra and then travels through the core of your body to the base chakra. From the base chakra, or base of your spine, it then travels down both of your legs, out through the soles of your feet and deep into the core of the Earth. Your Channel connects you to the nurturing source of energy that is our physical home in this life—our dazzlingly beautiful planet. The Channel also connects you to the highest possible level of your Divine Guidance, shining down into your crown and other chakras from the infinite realms of the Universe. Via your Channel, you become the connection point or junction between Heaven and Earth; a living, breathing receiver ready to bring light and enlightenment into your world.

A beam of light coming to you from the Cosmos, shining in through the top of your head and down through the core of your body—sounds familiar doesn't it? You just achieved it in exercise three, so you see that exercise's benefits are twofold—performing it will help you to clear and strengthen your Channel as well. You use your Channel to bring the light down to your chakras, and in doing so, also create a more powerful and receptive Channel. You're multitasking already; aren't you clever? And you thought this was going to be difficult.

Most people's Channels are weak and clogged at first; cluttered up with worry, fatigue, unresolved emotions, and negative ideas or thoughts. Like the chakras, the Channel is not a solid, physical organ like your heart or lungs. However, its healthy function is every bit as important.

Many times I have treated a client for a Channel that was damaged or unwell in some way and they have reported back to me their great feeling of relief and improved sense of wellbeing long after the healing was done. All manner of ailments, including depression, a lack of confidence, nausea, dizziness, and other physical complaints can be improved or relieved by clearing your Channel and keeping it strong.

As your Channel becomes healthier, you begin to notice other benefits, one of which is *automatically becoming more intuitive.* Once clear, your Channel is more open and free to bring you the information and guidance you desire.

For me, my Channel is an invaluable tool, the conduit for all my inspiration and the information I bring through for my clients. Here are some simple tips on how to clear and strengthen your own beautiful Channel.

REACTIVATING YOUR FULL CHANNEL

Requirement: A quiet location where you can sit or lie comfortably

Time required: 10–20 minutes

- Settle yourself comfortably and relax. Close your eyes when you are ready to begin.
- Imagine a beam of white light travelling down to you from way up in the Cosmos. Picture it travelling through the galaxies, into our solar system, and making a beeline for you here on planet Earth.
- Let the white light shine onto the top of your head, down through your head and neck, and then through the length of your body. This beam of light will be cylindrical in shape, like a pipe or tube, and flow through the centre of your body in front of your spine.
- Once it reaches your base chakra, let the white light branch out and continue to flow down through your hips and legs, passing through the upper legs, knees, lower legs, and ankles to the soles of your feet.
- From there, picture the white light reforming into one branch again and flowing down through the floor and into the earth, all the way to her core. Connecting your Channel to the earth's core is very important because it helps to keep you grounded.

Being clairvoyant is not about being "off in La-La Land," it is about bringing your Divine Guidance into your everyday, physical life.

- Sit for a moment and allow yourself to become reacquainted with the feeling of an active, connected, and energised Channel.

- Now you have the Universal white light flowing through you from top to bottom, connecting, through you, from the Cosmos to the core of the Earth. The next step gives you an even stronger connection to the Earth's nurturing energy. Note: Mother Earth is a soul and spirit in her own right and, as indigenous cultures have known for millennia, she is also the source of great wisdom. By tapping into her, we tap into a level of our own wisdom generally overlooked by western society.

- From the core of the earth, imagine a beautiful, rich, red light, the colour of a fine red wine, travelling back up towards you. Whilst the white light from above is vibrant and energising, the red light from the Earth is warm, comforting, and nurturing.

- Feel it flow up through the soles of your feet and moving all the way back up through your Channel—legs, hips, core of your body and head—until it flows up and out through your crown chakra and into the Cosmos.

- Keep breathing deeply and steadily, giving yourself a few moments to become reacquainted with this flow of energy.

- Now you have the white light flowing down through your Channel and the warm, red light flowing up. These two energies will flow simultaneously without getting in each others' way.

- After a few minutes, slowly open your eyes and reacquaint yourself with your surroundings. Your Channel will continue to be open and flowing.

- Repeat this exercise whenever you feel mentally or emotionally weakened or blocked; or any time you wish to strengthen your Channel.

What you have now is a fully functioning Channel that is probably more receptive than it's been since the earliest days of your childhood. Don't be dismayed if you didn't see or feel much on your first attempt, it will come with practice.

Working with our intuition is about learning to relax and let it happen, rather than making it happen. Your sensitivity will increase with practice.

Be aware that it's possible to have all kinds of mild reactions to the reawakening and clearing of your intuitive anatomy. Mild itching, tingling, or the sudden desire to laugh, cry, or yawn are all common. Some of you may feel a little unusually warm after working with this strong energy flow, this is perfectly normal and is a nice way to validate the change in your personal energy.

After you have done this exercise for the first time and reactivated your Channel, you may do this exercise daily so that you really get your Channel back into great shape and keep it that way. After ten years, I still use this technique regularly to keep my Channel strong.

Remember, one visit to the gym is good, but only regular visits will give you the results you desire, and just as the condition of your body improves with regular exercise, so too will the condition of your Channel.

The following are recommended maintenance exercises that can be done daily to maintain excellent Channel energy flow. Choose the one that you like best or alternate them to give yourself some added variety.

EXERCISE FIVE

CHANNEL MAINTENANCE TECHNIQUE
Breathing

Requirements: A quiet location where you can sit or lie comfortably

Time required: 5–10 minutes

- As with the previous exercise choose a quiet location and sit or lie comfortably.

- Begin by inhaling deeply. As you do so, visualise bringing the nurturing energy of the Earth up through your feet, legs, and body, and let it continue all the way up into the sky.

- With your out-breath visualise energy and light travelling down from the Universe via your Channel and through your entire body length, back down into the Earth.

- Do this several times and imagine that each inhalation and exhalation draws in more of this energy and light, helping to clear, expand, and strengthen your Channel.

- Repeat this exercise in reverse, drawing energy and light from the Universe on your in-breath and letting the Earth fill you up on the out-breath. Eventually you will be able to feel the energy moving in both directions simultaneously no matter where you are in your own breath cycle. This constant two-way flow is how your Channel functions naturally, and serves to keep you Divinely Guided and grounded all at the same time.

EXERCISE SIX

CHANNEL MAINTENANCE TECHNIQUE
Color and Light

Requirement: A quiet location where you can sit or lie comfortably

Time required: 5–10 minutes

- Make yourself comfortable and close your eyes.
- Visualise your Channel of pure white light.
- When ready, let your Channel be filled with a rich, bright colour. The first colour that comes to you is fine.
- Imagine this colour flowing down through your Channel from above, cleansing and strengthening it as it flows, letting it travel all the way to your feet and down into the Earth. Feel yourself being energised and uplifted by this wonderful, healing light, and ask that it bring you the Divine Guidance and spiritual connection you desire.
- Feel this coloured light come travelling back up through your Channel from the Earth, creating the continuous two-way flow. Remind yourself of your intention of clearing and strengthening your Channel by doing this exercise, and that's what will be done.

When it comes to the choice of colour, you are free to go with whatever you like. Many people see their favourite colours first, while others are drawn to colours that have a certain meaning for them. If you always see green, for instance, it could be that you need help with matters of the heart, as green is the main colour of the heart chakra; or it may simply be that green is a soothing and healing colour for you at that time. Try not to analyse things too much, and just let the healing powers of the energy and light do the work for you.

In my private work, my Angels often guide me to use brilliant gold and silver. Many times, the Angels have shown me how beneficial these powerful colours are for the purposes of healing and strengthening. When a client is particularly fatigued, I am often guided to use an energy that reminds me of champagne! It is a soft, golden colour, wonderfully sparkling and fresh. Such a colour is a great treat to give yourself when feeling a bit worn out.

In the end though, it is hard to go past a full rainbow. The entire band of colour is one of my favourites and is a delightful energy to work with. As you are practicing visualising and working on your Channel, simply call in a rainbow so that you may benefit from all the healing colours of the spectrum at once. Imagine a rainbow flowing in to the top of your head and down through the length of your Channel. Allow the individual colours to move through you, correcting any imbalances and dissolving any blockages as it goes.

Use one of these techniques for a few minutes each day and your Channel will remain strong and clear. Each time you practice, you will be fine-tuning your ability to receive your Divine Guidance in the many forms that it comes.

Your chakras will benefit enormously too, of course, and you'll feel refreshed and relaxed.

Now that you have set up the basics of your spiritual anatomy it is time to work on the really exciting part—activating your Inner Screen.

Your Inner Screen is connected to your brow chakra; its function is facilitating clairvoyant sight. The Inner Screen is a useful device because it gives your conscious mind something to focus on. Just closing your eyes and hoping for something to appear might be okay for some, but if you actually allow an Inner Screen to be formally created, your mind can go back to it each time with a positive and expectant air.

Remember, your intention is very important; creating an Inner Screen sets a clear intention of choosing to develop your clairvoyant sight once more.

EXERCISE SEVEN

CREATING THE INNER SCREEN

Requirements: A quiet location where you can sit or lie comfortably.

Time required: 10–15 minutes

- Close your eyes and focus on the inner surface of your brow.

- Let a stream of colour or light flow to this area and create a large, clear screen there for you inside your forehead. Don't try to see anything on your screen at this time, just imagine it being created and prepared for you in the most perfect way.

- Some of you will notice that this area feels thick or cloudy. Just like your Channel, the Inner Screen can become overwhelmed with worry, emotions, and the clutter and clatter of our minds. Ask the flow of colour and light to come and clear all of these obstructions away so that you can resurrect your clear Inner Screen.

- Utilise your imagination to help you picture a big white movie screen or flat screen plasma television on which you'll be able to see your images. Whenever I take a group of people through this exercise there are always a wonderful variety of Inner Screens.

- Have fun putting your Inner Screen together. Perhaps you imagine an elegant hand wiping the inner surface of your brow clear and clean. Or a cool breeze blowing away the old fog that the rational mind keeps in place in the form of scepticism, disbelief, or lack of confidence in your own abilities. You could even "invite" a famous person to come and unveil it by pulling a cord and drawing aside that inner curtain!

- There is no right or wrong way to do this exercise, so follow what feels good for you and trust that it is being done. In the beginning it may be difficult to see images like this clearly in your mind, so set your intention, give it your full attention, and do the best you can.

- Once you have cleaned your Inner Screen, slowly open your eyes and reconnect with your real environment, knowing that your Inner Screen is clear and ready to receive as needed.

- Allow yourself to feel confident that your Inner Screen is now clear and ready to help you develop your clairvoyant sight.

It is at this point that I would like to emphasise how important these simple exercises are. None of them need take very long, a couple of minutes a day can achieve wonders.

As you become more proficient you will be able to strengthen and clear your Channel, Inner Screen, and chakras at a moment's notice, whether you are sitting on a train or bus or taking a few minutes for yourself in the office.

Quiet time at home or in a meditation group is the ideal time and place, but if you are always "too busy," you must make time whenever you can. Your spiritual anatomy is similar to your physical anatomy in one very important way. If you look after it, use it, and treat it well, it'll remain healthy and strong and pay you back a thousandfold for your efforts.

CHAPTER FIVE

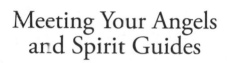

Meeting Your Angels
and Spirit Guides

In my experience, it is a rare person who isn't at least a little bit intrigued by the idea of meeting one of their Angels or Spirit Guides. I am fortunate enough to have travelled a great deal, and where ever I go I meet people who are hungry for more information on this subject.

Some people already have a strong belief about the existence of their unseen friends, others have felt a loving presence around them before, particularly during a difficult time in their lives. It is natural for many more people to be sceptical; after all, we live in a world where physical or actual proof of a thing's existence is usually the minimum standard.

Recently I had the good fortune to go to Rome and enjoy the monumental and beautiful works of art that cover the walls and ceilings of the Vatican buildings and the Sistine Chapel. There, it struck me how angels have long been depicted in art, but usually in scenes of great drama, triumph, or religious significance. Perhaps the underlying message that we have taken from this is that angels only come to you if you are someone special, or that they belong only in the mythologies of certain religions. Thankfully today we are broadening our view to the point where thousands of people are now happy to confess their interest in and experiences with their Angels and Spirit Guides.

Many people ask me what the difference is between Spirit Guides, Angels, Archangels, and Ascended Masters, as they are the four "levels" of beings that I most commonly Channel during the readings.

The way it has been explained and shown to me over the years is that each of these groups live in a different dimension or vibration. The vibration in which the Spirit Guides live is closest to our dimension here on Earth, or to put it another way, it has a similar frequency.

All Spirit Guides have lived on Earth before as human beings, giving them a profound understanding of what our experiences here are like. When we are born we have some Spirit Guides with us, some of whom will stay with us for the duration of our lives and some who will only be here for the time it takes to help us to get the most from certain human experiences we come here to understand.

Therefore the number of Spirit Guides a person can have with them at any one time will vary, as new ones come and old ones leave depending on where you are in life.

I can vividly recall the positive effect that connecting with a Spirit Guide had for one of my clients who was going through a difficult time. In her midthirties and never married, this lady was devastated by the death of both her parents within the same year. When she first came to see me she felt very alone, and realised that she had given little thought or energy to getting married—her parents and her career had always been of paramount importance to her.

She often cried herself to sleep at night, wondering when it would be her turn and realising that her inherent shyness had caused her to avoid making contact with eligible men. Her somewhat sheltered life had changed forever and she needed help.

She had a general sense of her Spirit Guides from her first session with me, so we called on them again and asked them for help. Soon after, as she lay crying in bed one night, she felt a warm presence surround her and a sense of calm descend in her mind. She reported a soothing sensation as though someone were stroking the side of her face lovingly and brushing the hair from her tear-streaked face, it was very comforting and reassuring for her.

This experience continued most nights for the next few months. Feeling lonely in her empty home, she spoke to this Spirit Guide and told him of her feelings and fears. She came to think of him as Tom, was very sure that he was male, and could describe his appearance. As she recovered from her grief she also came to think of him as a constant friend.

Then one day this woman realised that she had not seen Tom for quite a while. Her life had become so busy and it had been several months since she had given her

Spirit Guides and Angels any thought at all. She felt a bit guilty, remembering how much Tom's visits had meant to her. On thinking about it further she realised that he had not shown himself since something very special had happened in her life.

During these last few months she had finally begun to notice the attentions of a male coworker. He had always been very nice to her, but she never thought much of it. One day he asked her out for lunch and during their conversation it suddenly hit her—she liked him very much and always had, but had remained closed to him.

The relationship blossomed rapidly from there and soon they were engaged, and both truly delighted. It suddenly occurred to her that Tom had been there to help her through that lonely time after her parents' death and to listen to her feelings about wanting her own relationship and family.

Our connection with our Spirit Guides and Angels can be funny that way; we might only think of them when we are in trouble and then "forget" them when the problem is solved. They don't mind, because they understand that emotional pain is a bit like physical pain, you don't notice the part of you that is hurting after the pain is gone.

Because your Spirit Guides come and go, so to speak, it is always worth checking in from time to time to see who's with you. I was recently introduced to a new one of my own, and working with him and getting to know him has been delightful.

Many, but not all, Angels, so they tell me, have also lived on Earth. Those who haven't lived here still have the gift of empathy and relate to us very well. All Angels bring a wider perspective of understanding to our lives. The vibration, frequency, or dimension that they dwell in is of a higher tone. This doesn't mean they are better than Spirit Guides or humans, but they have a different view and understanding. It is common for Angels to let a client know they are learning just as much from us as we are from them.

We benefit our Angels by allowing them to help us because that is an important part of their mission. In my experience, the number of Angels with any one person remains consistent throughout their lifetime, with some Angels taking a more prominent role at various times. Our Angels have known us since before we were born, and helped us choose the kind of incarnation that would be of most benefit to our soul's purpose in this life.

Naturally, they are also here to help us, but unless our parents were enlightened enough to teach us about their presence, most of us completely forget about our Angels by the time we reach puberty.

Your parents were probably inclined to tell you that it was just your imagination when you reported the awareness of one of your Angels as a child. Fortunately this trend is changing as more adults come to experience

Angelic presence as truth, and help to keep this knowledge alive in their children.

There doesn't seem to be any limit to the number of Spirit Guides or Angels that you can have in your personal group, some people have a veritable crowd around them, but you will certainly have all that you need whether you are aware of them or not.

Archangels and Ascended Masters inhabit different realms and having been Angels and/or Spirit Guides in previous incarnations; they are very experienced and powerful. Both of these groups are omnipresent, which means that they are available to anyone and everyone at all times. These beings are of such a high vibration that just thinking about one of them can bring comfort and give your own vibe a boost.

The Archangels Michael, Gabriel, Raphael, and Uriel are familiar to most of you by name at least, but there are many more. The Ascended Masters are an impressive group including among them no less than Mother Mary, Mary Magdalene, Jesus (Lord Sananda), Joseph of Arimathea, Saint Germaine, Lady Nada, and Lord Kuthumi. For the purposes of this book however, we will focus only on your own personal group, your Spirit Guides and Angels. If you're curious about the Archangels and Ascended Masters, I encourage you to do your own research, and see where it takes you.

Over the years I have spoken to many people who felt they had been protected or saved by a force outside of themselves when they were placed in a dangerous situation. One man I met a long time ago was in a horrendous car accident in the New Zealand countryside. A split second before the accident happened, he saw a brilliant flash of light and had a profound feeling that everything was going to be all right despite the chaos all around him

The memory of that light helped him to remain positive and strong as he went through his long recovery. Ultimately he came to understand that the changes the accident had brought about in his life were positive, and he felt extremely thankful.

I have also had a number of encounters with helpful Angels who came to comfort or help me. One such visit happened only a few years ago; by which time I was already very accustomed to having them around. It was a very hot summer, early February if my memory serves me right, and a friend in Brisbane was unable to locate his very old and feeble cat.

This cat was a beloved pet, close to twenty years old. It was not handling the +40°C heat wave well at all. At about ten PM, my friend phoned me to say that he had searched *everywhere* for this cat and was extremely worried—he didn't want her to suffer.

My clairvoyant sight revealed nothing to me. We chatted for a while, said our farewells, and I went off to bed. After lying with my eyes closed for around fifteen minutes, I felt an urge to open my eyes. At the end of my bed stood three enormous Angels. They were of a soft, whitish, cloud-like outline, all of them male and very strong looking—very masculine. Instinctively I felt that they were the Archangels Gabriel, Raphael, and Michael, and the energy of their presence was calming, reassuring, and wonderful.

The whole meeting lasted no more than ten seconds. I watched them as they stood there looking not so much at me, but more like through or around me. Immediately I had a strong feeling that my friend's cat would be found alive and well; the Angels then disappeared and off to sleep I went.

The following morning a very excited email came from my friend letting me know that he had found his cat sleeping under the house in a place my friend thought he had already searched, twenty to thirty minutes after we ended our phone conversation. I was delighted of course, and had yet another good reason to say thanks to the Angels.

Okay, I know you're keen to discover how it is you can connect with your wonderful friends. The following exercise is simple, effective, and a great way to meet with your Angels and Spirit Guides.

Before you start the exercise, make it your clear intention that this is what you want. If the idea of having Angels and Spirit Guides around you is completely new, you may feel a little bit nervous, but there is nothing to worry about. Make it your intention to connect with these beings who love you and have your best interests at heart.

Make sure that you have done all the previous exercises from chapter four at least once before moving on to this process.

This book is presented in a certain order for a reason, so until you have done each exercise at least once, it is best that you follow the sequence as it is presented, just as you would do if you were taking one of my courses and learning something new each week in class.

After you have done them all, starting with the chakra maintenance, Channel, and Inner Screen activations from chapter four, you can pick and choose which exercises appeal to you most and focus more upon them.

I also recommend that you get yourself a notebook or journal in which you can keep a record of the experiences you will have and the information you will receive. It's easy to forget the details when your mind gets busy again, and far too easy to lose the well meaning scrap of paper you scribbled on. Treat yourself to a lovely book to record your adventures; it will be well worth it.

EXERCISE EIGHT

MEET ONE OF YOUR ANGELS OR SPIRIT GUIDES

Requirements: A quiet place where you can sit or lie
   comfortably
   Pen or pencil
   Notebook or journal

Time required: 10–20 minutes

- First sit or lie down somewhere you can be comfortable, take the phone off the hook, put the "Do Not Disturb" sign out, anything you need to ensure you won't be interrupted. It is probably best not to do this in bed because the object of this exercise is not to fall asleep, nor is it necessarily to relax—you want to be calm and focused and ready to connect.
- Spend a couple of minutes doing the Channel activation process from chapter four, so that you know your Channel is open and strong. Remember, your Channel is your antenna for your Divine Guidance, so the more exercise you give it, the better it will work for you.
- Have your pen and notebook within reach.
- Now close your eyes and take a moment to consider your intention, the reason you are doing this exercise—to meet one of your Spirit Guides or Angels.
- Imagine yourself travelling up into the sky. Floating or flying, you leave your room behind and fly up through the sky, going higher and higher. Imagine the clouds as you pass them by. You feel happy, free, and full of excited anticipation.
- Imagine your Channel to be like a kind of guide rope that guides you on your journey up into space while still keeping you safely connected to Earth.

- Soon you notice you've risen so far that you begin to leave the Earth's atmosphere and are moving out into space.

- Picture yourself going past our beautiful moon and out past the planets in our solar system such as Venus, Jupiter, Neptune, and Pluto. Make your journey as colourful and interesting as you like, there is no need to rush. Stop and study the awesome and colourful rings of Saturn, or marvel at the comets and asteroids as they glide on by. Note: If you want to be really thorough you can take the time to look at an atlas of astronomy or the internet to familiarise yourself with the celestial geography before you head off, so you can picture where you are going with greater ease.

- Continue to travel upward into the Cosmos, holding your clear intention in your mind that you are on a journey to meet one of your Angels or Spirit Guides. Soon you will leave our solar system and find yourself in the vastness of space where you will continue to travel for a minute or two longer, enjoying the incredible peace of the Universe and the brilliance of the stars.

- When you feel ready, allow yourself to come to a stop and to simply float or hover in space with stars and planets moving slowly around you.

- Pause for a moment and let yourself feel the security of the guideline and anchor your Channel provides for you.

- Now that you have become a little bit accustomed to just "hanging out" in space, look straight ahead into the distance and imagine a small but very bright point of light. Let this light come closer and closer to you. It travels with great speed and accuracy, becoming larger all the while.

- Eventually it is right there before you, only a few feet away, and so very bright that you may feel the urge to shield your eyes. Remind yourself that you are here to meet a Spirit Guide or Angel, a meeting that, one way or another, you have been looking forward to all your life. You will soon notice that the intensity of this mass of light begins to soften a little so that you are able to look directly at it.

- As you watch, a form will begin to reveal itself to you; there is nothing you have to do other than just observe. Just relax and allow your Angel or Spirit Guide to come to you. Be receptive and welcoming, and notice whatever shows up.

- You may get a sense of whether it is male or female, or notice part or all of his or her appearance, and so on. In your mind's eye let the image of your Angel or Spirit Guide be shown to you and keep asking for more information. It is perfectly acceptable to ask as many questions as you like, especially if you are not very visual at this time.

- Ask your guide what colour its eyes are, what it's wearing, its name, or whether it is an Angel or a Spirit Guide. Even if you can't see this being, you will feel it. Its energy feels warm and wonderful, so you may want to reach out to hold hands or give and receive a hug.

- Keep examining your Spirit Guide or Angel until you've gathered all the information about them you can at this time. Trust what you sense and let the impressions flow freely—your friend can have any name and any kind of appearance. Not all Angels have flowing robes and golden wings and Spirit Guides appear in a truly limitless variety.

- When you feel you've spent enough time with your friend, you can then make your journey back to Earth—this time with your Spirit Guide or Angel by your side.

- Using your Channel as a guiding line again, travel back down along it through the stars, into our solar system and back into the Earth's atmosphere. Picture yourself descending gently and gracefully with your Spirit Guide or Angel by your side and going directly back to where ever you began your journey.

- Make your journey back logical and sequential, coming back the same way you went out, then returning to the country, city, town, suburb, street, home or building, and then finally the room you set out from.

Affirm to yourself the present place and time; for example, your street address and the date. Breathe deeply, wriggle your fingers and toes, feel the weight of your body in the chair, and open your eyes. You are back where you started and your Angel or Spirit Guide is now beside you.

• Before you do anything else, take your pen and notebook and write down every little detail you can remember, including a name if you received one. It really helps to make a note of these things when you are in the early stages of this work because it is all too easy to leap back into your busy day and forget half of what you experienced. This whole process need only take a few minutes if that is what you want, but if you can spare the time it is worthwhile giving yourself around half an hour so you can savour and enjoy it.

If at any time during the process you feel you've drifted off, just pick up where you left off. There is no right or wrong way to do this, so you may add your own variations if you like. Some people like to imagine that they are walking into a beautiful forest, stopping in a clearing or a grove to meet their new friend. If you have a favourite place or setting you would prefer to use, then by all means do so. No one method is better than the other; what is most important is that it works for you.

Normally, you will meet just one Angel or Spirit Guide each time you make this trip, but it's possible to be greeted by two or more. There are no rules, so be open to surprises and trust yourself and what you are being shown. Keep asking the ones you connect with for the names they go by; I find it is much easier for people to relate to an Angel or Spirit Guide if they have a name to address them by. There don't seem to be any names that are typical; in my ten years of practice I have come across Spirit Guides and Angels with names ranging from the very ordinary, like Bob and Jane, to the unusual, like Wohan and Erethelia.

Once you have made contact there is no need to repeat that process again for the same Angel or Spirit Guide, but do repeat it whenever you would like to meet other members of your clan. If you are going through a difficult time, or want help with something specific, you can ask to meet the being who can most particularly help you with that problem. You may then be guided to a new one or be shown which of your known Angels or Spirit Guides can help you.

STAYING IN TOUCH
WITH YOUR GUIDES

Getting to know your Angels or Guides better is also a simple process. Develop your relationship with them by talking to them in your mind. Start your day by inviting them to join you and be close to you, say "Good morning, Erethelia. Thank you for this wonderful day. Please come and be close by my side throughout the day, and please help me with …" and so on.

Ask your Angels and Spirit Guides to reveal more about themselves to you in your relaxed and quiet times. Make time to sit and commune with them or contemplate them as you are drifting off to sleep. If you didn't get a name during that initial process then keep asking for it and it will come to you eventually.

Your Angels and Spirit Guides want to have a closer relationship with you, so tell them about yourself, your life, how you feel, and what you dream of. It's all about getting reacquainted with a long-lost friend—there's a lot of catching up to do, so don't hold back.

Messages from your new friends can come to you in all sorts of ways. Say for instance you are getting frustrated because you can't seem to determine your Angel's name. If you expect the name to come to you like some booming voice in your head, you may be missing the point.

Sure, the booming voice can happen, just like it does in the movies, but what's more likely is that you will have a feeling or a sense of a name; a more subtle impression rather than something that knocks you off your chair.

Your celestial friends will also use everyday items and situations to communicate with you, so it's important to be observant, like my client who kept asking her Angel for his name. In frustration, she rang me and said, "Maybe he doesn't want to tell me his name." After she hung up, she left for work.

That day in the office, the name Daniel kept coming to her from all over the place. She was introduced to someone called Daniel, two customer enquiries that she had to deal with were from people named Daniel, and finally, as she was driving home, the car in front of her in the slow moving, peak hour traffic had a customised number plate with the letters "DAN" on it. She finally got it and laughed about it all the way home.

Your Angels and Spirit Guides will find all sorts of interesting and creative ways to communicate with you and to help you to develop your faith in their presence. They have an amazing sense of timing and humour, with an approach that will often serve to remind us to slow down and enjoy life rather than constantly rushing around getting things done. One of their most commonly acknowledged methods is to leave feathers in the most unusual places for you, like a calling card to remind you that they are around. Or you might see a feather lying in a fairly normal location like a park, but it will really grab your attention.

Their messages can come to you in any way, shape, or form, so be observant and don't be surprised if a song you have heard a thousand times suddenly holds new meaning for you, if people keep mentioning similar ideas or themes to you in conversation, or if the headline on the next magazine or newspaper you pick up makes sense to you in a very personal way. Your Angels and Spirit Guides will use whatever means are at hand because they know all too well that our minds are often too busy to clearly hear spoken messages.

Over time you will learn to notice and respond to the more subtle forms of contact like that inner feeling or nudge that your Angels or Spirit Guides will give you to help you make the most positive choices for yourself.

Tuning in to these subtle messages takes practice and a willingness to be patient with yourself as you learn to let go of the lifelong habit of overriding your intuitive feelings.

It is important to realise that even though we have a lot of different languages here on Earth, the Universe doesn't communicate in any of them as such. The real language of the soul is one of feeling, so if something feels right, believe and act on it. Likewise, when it doesn't feel right, don't. It really is that simple.

One of the most effective ways to allow your Angels and Spirit Guides to help you is to speak to them from a place of intention and empowerment. The old approach of asking for something in a "please give me this/please make such and such happen/please do this and that for me" manner is no longer very effective.

As part of humanity's overall evolutionary process we are being encouraged to take responsibility and control over the creation of our own reality. There is no "God" on high, dispensing wishes to some and not to others. We need to learn to take responsibility for the fact that we create and attract most of what we experience in our lives.

To this end, a much better way of making "requests" of any kind is to word it this way: "Dear Angels, what do I need to do or not do, start or stop, understand, embrace or let go of, in order to bring this into my life, in order to have this experience? What can I do to help this desired event come about, and how can I allow myself to receive (whatever it is you are asking for)?"

Do you notice the difference? You are not making a passive plea for help and expecting the Universe to sort it all out for you. You are activating the powerful energy of your intention and indicating to your Spirit Guides, Angels, and the Universe that you are willing to do your share and meet halfway.

When you communicate with your celestial friends in this way, it gives them much greater scope to help you by creating situations and opportunities that bring your wishes to life. By actively calling your friends' attention to you in this way you will be co-creating your life with their help, and have the chance to make changes and choices that will help you to refine the outcome.

Becoming more intuitive and clairvoyant is not about waiting around for someone else to fix your life for you; it's about working with your helpers to develop your own innate skills and strengths as the powerful, spiritually aware being that you are and are becoming.

You can use this method to request help with less tangible matters as well. You may, for instance, wish to develop qualities you feel you lack, such as courage, compassion, confidence, or faith in yourself. To ask your

Angels "How can I develop a greater faith in myself? What do I need to do or not do, learn or let go of," and the like is a very empowering experience, and will generate some incredible opportunities for you.

At first, you may not recognise your Angels' response to your request until you look back and think, "Wow! I felt really strong in that situation, and stuck to my guns. That was a great opportunity to develop my faith in myself!"

One last advantage of working with your Spirit Guides and Angels in this way is you find out very quickly what you *really* want. It is all very well to bombard your Angels with a shopping list that says "Give me this, this, this, and this," but when you bring yourself into the equation and acknowledge that you must meet the Universe halfway and act in your own best interests, you soon weed out the things that aren't so important to you. This then frees you to focus on what you *really* desire for yourself and your life. You will find that when a genuine request is made from the heart, with a willingness to participate, the Universe always responds.

CHAPTER SIX

How to Conduct a Psychic Conversation

I don't know about you, but throughout my life I have found it difficult at times to communicate my true feelings to someone. Fortunately I have usually been able to let someone know when I like, love, and appreciate them; though maybe not often enough. What I am talking about are those difficult conversations where the subject matter is tricky or liable to trigger some kind of disagreement or conflict.

Like most people, I would rather run a mile across burning hot coals than confront someone. For much of my life, I felt intimidated by most people, *especially* those whom I perceived to have a temper and be capable of expressing their anger openly toward me.

This was terrifying stuff for me and I would avoid it at all costs; but as we know, this does not usually lead to a resolution and can often make matters worse.

Ideally I guess it would be wonderful if we could all be composed and courageous enough to take our concerns or confusion directly to the person involved and discuss it with them face to face. We have all beaten ourselves up in the past for not being "more adult" about things. If you feel this way, remind yourself that verbal and even written communication are known to be only partially effective and are open to misinterpretation.

This is where the technique of the Psychic Conversation can be extremely useful because it is a tool which can help you communicate with other people effectively and gently.

The term "psychic" in this case does not refer to someone with a gift for reading the future or tapping into another person's thoughts or beliefs. What it refers to is a mode of communication other than a physical or verbal one. It refers to the fact that we communicate with each other on much more subtle levels all the time, mostly without even knowing it. In fact, observers and researchers in the field of human communication have long acknowledged that speech constitutes only around ten percent of all interpersonal communication.

We communicate much more eloquently with each other through our body language, our facial expressions, our actions and our *thoughts*. If you believe that you can be angry or upset with someone and hide it from them because you haven't actually told them about it, then you are fooling yourself. Human beings are incredibly sensitive, and even if the object of your anger or hurt can't accurately describe the vibe you are giving off, he or she will know something is amiss.

A Psychic Conversation is effective because you are communicating with more than words and thoughts— you are also using your feelings. It doesn't matter what language you speak or what generation you are from; as human beings, we all understand the power and energy of feelings because they bypass our mind (which is likely to filter and interpret them), and they reach us in our heart and our gut.

Psychic Conversations are also a great help when the person you want to communicate with lives far away.

Phone calls, letters, emails, and the like are notorious for being open to misinterpretation over long distances and/or when you haven't seen the person for quite some time.

So if you balk at the idea of fronting up to a certain person with a request or a problem, if you know that your voice will shake, or your bottom lip will quiver or that you are liable to burst into tears and forget half the things you wanted to say, don't feel bad. You are not being weak, you are simply being human.

Or if like me, you sometimes find yourself suffering from a bad case of "foot-in-mouth" disease when trying to communicate your feelings, fear not: help is at hand. All of us are sensitive to the reactions and opinions of others. Getting the words to come out correctly whilst under pressure can be difficult.

Sometimes it seems as though the world is full of people who would like us to believe they can intimidate us into having things their way. The wonderful thing about Psychic Conversation is that it allows you to approach someone you might even be afraid of, and get a positive result. It can turn supposed enemies into friends, intimidators into supporters, resolve issues with people who no longer belong in your life so you can let them go, and give you a sense of inner strength you did not previously know you had.

It is worth noting here that the Psychic Conversation technique is not about forcing others to come around to your point of view, it is about giving yourself the best possible opportunity of expressing your truth clearly without the interruption or even derision you may fear. The Psychic Conversation was taught to me by my Angels and Guides many years ago, not as a tool to be used up front, before I had given the other person a chance, but to be used when all my other attempts at communicating my feelings or needs had failed. When it was very clear the other person would not be open to hearing or considering my point of view, I would prepare for a Psychic Conversation.

It is not a tool that you can use to manipulate others; it cannot influence them unfairly to do what you want, it is simply another way of communicating with someone, a way that most of us have forgotten or are reluctant to acknowledge.

By having Psychic Conversations with people, you are able to communicate with them on a very deep and direct level, and you will be able to express yourself clearly and fully without fear of interruption or negative reaction.

Once I learned the technique of the Psychic Conversation, I realised that I had been having lesser versions of these types of conversations with people all my life. We all do it.

Just think about this for a moment: if someone upsets you, is keeping something from you, forgets your birthday or wedding anniversary or something like that, what do you do? Chances are you will play the scene over in your head countless times, imagining yourself handling the situation with more courage or calm. You will rerun a type of conversation in your mind, going over how you feel and what you want, usually going around in circles until you are fed up with the whole thing, and yet after all this effort and stress on your part, the situation remains unresolved. The process is disempowering because you are doing it from a place of powerlessness. All you're really doing is chewing on the angst that you feel and making matters worse for yourself. Learning how to conduct a Psychic Conversation will change all that.

The Psychic Conversation uses the incredible power of our conscious and subconscious minds to create a constructive communication which honours and respects for all involved. By focusing your attention on the person and the difficulty at hand, you can resolve situations that may otherwise remain stuck for long periods of time. The Psychic Conversation gives you the opportunity to communicate with others at the level of the heart, a level of much greater openness and deeper understanding, and because you are able to concentrate fully on your own feelings and what you want to communicate, it is a very effective process.

Often when we try to communicate with others in ordinary ways—such as verbally or in writing—we encounter barriers constructed by the other person at the level of the ego and conscious mind. For better or for worse we have all grown up to believe that we have to defend our corner in life, and that understanding another's needs or point of view is a form of weakness that leaves us open to losing in some way.

Growing up in a complex and competitive world, our defences are strong; *all* of us have and use them. The Psychic Conversation is not about drumming in to the other person that you are right and he/she is wrong, it is a tool to be used respectfully so that you can express your true feelings without censure or interruption.

My Angels taught me a "three strikes, you're out" policy with Psychic Conversations I believe is very useful. If you have the same Psychic Conversation with the same person three times and still get no response, then it's time to accept that the other party is simply not interested in your point of view, and move on. You have used the tool with integrity, expressed your feelings clearly, and described in detail the outcome you would like, but what other people on the receiving end do with this kind of communication is always up to them. We are all beings of free will and are not here to spend our time and energy trying to force others to bend to ours; by acknowledging the "three strikes, you're out" policy, you are showing that you are humble and flexible enough to let go and move on.

The Psychic Conversation technique has brought me some amazing responses and results, and has proven to me without a doubt that we can communicate with others at the level of thought, without even being in the same country, city, or room.

After conducting a Psychic Conversation with people, I have received phone calls or bumped into them on the street, sometimes after not having seen them for years. Not only have they contacted me, but they have then initiated a discussion about the exact topic of my concern. Sometimes they'll come forth with an apology or offer important information depending on what I asked for as the outcome.

A classic example is my experience of being awarded a pay rise in my job during my time in the fashion industry. My boss had made it clear to all of us that no pay rises would be forthcoming in the foreseeable future, but I knew that compared to my colleagues, I was being considerably underpaid. I found my boss very intimidating in those days, and there was no way I was game to broach this subject with him, but after conducting two Psychic Conversations with him on this topic, a miracle happened.

About a week after the second conversation I was summoned to his office. I had no idea what this meeting was going to be about, as I had forgotten about my Psychic

Conversation efforts. You can imagine my surprise and delight when he told me I would be receiving a pay rise.

He made it very clear to me that I was to tell nobody about it; company policy was not permitting pay rises at this time, but he had been aware that I had been working hard, had started on a lower salary than my peers due to my initial lack of experience in my role, and that I had not had a pay rise since I'd started. My boss had gotten permission from the owner of the company to give me a rise of $5000 a year!

I was thrilled and could barely suppress my urge to laugh. It was hard to keep my good news to myself, but I thanked my Angels a hundred times that day for their help. My Psychic Conversation with my boss had worked, the evidence could not be denied.

Another striking example was during a time when I was dating a man with whom I was quite taken. He was an instructor at my gym, and with the benefit of hindsight I might say now that I should've known better.

He and I dated for a while and it was all very nice, but after a couple of months I couldn't shake the feeling that something wasn't right. He would behave a bit strangely from time to time, get phone calls at odd hours that seemed to vex him, and would sometimes cancel a date on very short notice.

Naturally I wasn't impressed and had tried to talk to him about it, but he would just clam up or say I was overreacting. I had no actual proof of any deceit or wrongdoing, but my intuition told me something was very wrong. Now you need to remember that I really liked this guy at the time, and at the basic level of ego, I wanted to believe that everything was okay. He was a gym instructor and personal trainer after all—a busy guy, always in demand!

Some of my friends were suspicious of his behaviour, but most of them believed I was reading too much into things and that I should just relax or be more patient. But I finally listened to my intuition, and decided to have a Psychic Conversation with him in order to find out where we stood.

The outcome I wanted was him being honest with me about what was going on in his life, so I could make an informed choice about my involvement with him. Once again, the result was much better and swifter in coming than I had expected. He phoned me the following morning to say that he wanted to see me as soon as I was able He came around to my place for a late breakfast, and without any prompting, he confessed all.

It turned out that he wasn't ready for a relationship at all, and that although he had been trying to start a relationship with me, he had not completely gotten over his previous girlfriend, and was still in the throes of trying to either patch things up or let things go completely; the situation was complicated and messy. No woman ever feels terribly flattered by this kind of revelation. It's not a very glamorous thing to find out that you are the rebound girl, but at least I had the truth and could end our relationship without any doubts in my mind.

Although it initially hurt to hear the truth, the Psychic Conversation had brought me a good result, as I was then able to make an informed decision and move on.

So, by now I hope you are bouncing up and down in your seats demanding "How do I conduct one of these Psychic Conversations?!"

Here's how: read the instructions carefully and keep it simple. This isn't a complicated process. The most important thing is that you are coming from a genuine place of integrity, and have already tried discussing your concern with the person with whom you want to have a Psychic Conversation.

Your intention is everything, and is all important to receiving a positive and helpful response. If your intention is just to ram your opinion down the other person's throat, to fire off blame for your unhappiness, or to try to prove yourself right, the Universe won't support you. The Psychic Conversation is not a place for righteous indignation or a cheap attempt at manipulating the will or behaviour of others. Make sure your intention is purely to express your true feelings in a clear and honest manner.

On some occasions, your part of the conversation will include feelings of anger or disappointment, or letting the other person know you didn't like what was said or done, but it's not about making someone else 'fess up to being wrong, it's about owning your feelings on the matter. In the Psychic Conversation, you are creating the chance to express exactly what you want.

CONDUCTING A PSYCHIC
CONVERSATION

Requirements A quiet location where you can sit or lie
comfortably
A clear intention

Time required: Approximately 20 minutes

- First of all, decide who it is you want to talk to and
what your main topic will be.

- Sit or lie somewhere quiet, comfortable, and private.
Close your eyes. Calm your mind and focus on your
intention, including the outcome you would like to
have happen as a result of this conversation.

- Imagine yourself contacting this person in some
way, by telephone for example, and calmly inform
him or her that you wish to talk. Designate the time
and place. Make sure it is a place where you feel very
comfortable, confident, and safe, such as a favourite
café, park, beach, or your own living room if you
prefer. Anywhere that you can imagine talking with
this person about your chosen topic is fine.

- Imagine them arriving just as you have instructed.
Welcome them and have them place themselves
wherever you want.
Begin by clearly stating your topic, then tell them
everything you have not been able to tell them so far.

Imagine them sitting and listening to you respectfully and attentively; simply taking in what you are
saying without reaction. Go into as much detail as
you want and need to. Say everything you need to
say and get it all off your chest. This is your time to
speak—you have created this opportunity to do it,
so use it well.

• When you are completely finished, be sure to then
  say what *outcome* you want. You will have thought
  about his clearly before starting the Psychic Conversation, but if other ideas come to you while it
  is happening that's fine. Don't leave anything out.
  Would you like an apology? How about a phone call
  from that person or an offer to renew the friendship? Maybe you want to reconcile with your partner, and had an apology of your own to offer during
  the conversation; or maybe it is a pay rise you want.
  Make sure that your desired outcome is very clear.

• After you've completely expressed your feelings
  about your side of the situation and have been clear
  about the outcome you'd like, you can then thank the
  person for coming and hearing you. Next, politely
  ask him or her to leave. The other person does not
  reply or respond, remember, they are a being of free
  will, so it is not for you to try to imagine what they
  might say. The meeting you've just had was initiated
  by *you* and was *your* opportunity to talk.

- Once the person has left, continue to sit peacefully with your eyes closed for a few moments. Notice how you are feeling after having expressed yourself clearly and truthfully. Let that feeling sink in. When you are ready, open your eyes.

- If you wish, jot down the details of who you spoke to, what you said, and what outcome you requested.

After conducting a Psychic Conversation, most people report feeling a sense of relief or lightness because they have finally found a constructive way to release something they've been carrying around inside themselves for a while.

It is now up to the other person to respond, and time for you to let go, because you cannot control anyone but yourself. The best thing you can do after the end of the Psychic Conversation is forget about it and carry on with your life.

If you believe you're dealing with a particularly stubborn or resistant person, you may have the same or similar conversation with them up to a total of three times.

Sometimes the response will come to you in ways you hadn't imagined. You may well get the apology you wanted, but it may come in the form of a letter or card, or through a third party, rather than in person or on the phone as you might have expected.

Understand that you are learning a new way of communicating with people, and like all new skills, this one will also benefit you more with practice. Be patient with yourself and allow space for your desired outcome to happen in miraculous ways.

One of the most striking memories of a Psychic Conversation I have was of helping one of my students years ago, during one of the many meditation courses I used to run.

A young woman was being hounded by her ex-boyfriend. She had broken up with him several months before joining our group, but she was quiet in class and I knew nothing of her situation. On the night I took the students through the Psychic Conversation technique, she worked through the process like everyone else did, and we all parted ways without incident.

It was not my policy to inquire as to the content of each student's conversation, but only to help them with the process if they didn't understand something or felt stuck.

The following week, we all gathered for class and I asked if anyone had a story to share after trying the Psychic Conversation technique for the first time. The quiet young woman offered to share hers.

Many of us were very troubled by her description of her ex-boyfriend's behaviour; she had ended the relationship because he became verbally abusive when he drank alcohol. He would yell, slam doors, and storm out. They had received many complaints from their neighbours. It had been hard for her to end things. When the man was sober, he promised it would never happen again and he would be "on his best behaviour" for a while, but refused to seek any professional help, even though she had made it clear she was willing to support him through it.

When she finally found the strength to end it for good, she moved out of the home they had shared together and rented her own place. After a month or so, he discovered her new address and started harassing her.

She'd already had to change the number of her mobile phone due to his persistent phone calls, but when he started turning up outside her apartment at all hours banging on the door, and waiting outside her place of work, it all became too much.

She told us she put all the energy and emotion she could muster into her Psychic Conversation, and allowed herself to say all the things to him she had been frightened to say before. Her desired outcome had been made very clear—she wanted him to leave her alone and was beyond the point of even hoping for any kind of apology.

Three days after her Psychic Conversation with her ex, she found a hand-written letter from him in her letterbox. Her first impulse was to throw it away out of fear, assuming it would contain more of the abuse and accusations that had become commonplace from him. To her relief and amazement, the letter was a long and emotional apology ending in a promise to never contact or try to find her again.

She had put the Psychic Conversation out of her mind and gotten on with her very busy life; she had a demanding job in IT and worked long hours. Like most people, she was a little bit sceptical, and didn't seriously expect much to happen. Having gone into the process with the attitude that it might help and wouldn't do any harm, she had not been sitting around waiting for something cataclysmic to happen. As is so often the case when we do our share of the "work" and then let it go, the Universe had delivered something that far exceeded her expectations.

The young woman continued to take part in the meditation classes for several months and stayed in contact as a private client, and I'm confident that she never heard from or saw her ex-boyfriend again.

The technique of the Psychic Conversation is something you can easily learn. Following the instructions from earlier will get you started.

Some people like to light a candle or call on their Angels to help them before starting; whatever works for you is just fine. As far as your conscious mind is concerned, the Psychic Conversation will be taking place in your head. The difference is that when you put your positive intention behind your actions and your honest emotion and feeling into those actions, you will be communicating from your heart. The person on the receiving end may not like or agree with what you have to say, but when something is done with integrity and honesty, it cannot be ignored or dismissed.

Sometimes the outcome of a Psychic Conversation is simply for both parties to "agree to disagree," which is an opportunity for your feelings to be aired even though the relationship is over. At other times however, Pyschic Conversation outcomes can facilitate the creation of very positive changes, stronger understanding, and deep bonds.

So go ahead and enjoy yourself as you learn to use this process. Remember you can use the Psychic Conversation for "good" things too! If someone in your life whom you adore is a bit prickly and difficult to reach (whether physically or metaphorically), you can use the Psychic Conversation to remind the person of your love.

CHAPTER SEVEN

The Art of Automatic Writing

Automatic writing is one of the most effective ways to work with and strengthen your clairvoyant connection. It's another form of channelling—one that really helps you to feel the difference between receiving your Divine Guidance as compared to your usual train of thought.

Recording the guidance that comes to and through you is also an excellent way to capture the flow of information as it happens. In recording, messages become permanent records for you to look over again whenever you want. It's very easy to forget what's been seen or said, or for other people to interpret events differently, but when you write something down as it comes to you in the moment, it provides you with a wonderful record not only of the information you've received, but of your increasing clarity as you practice over time.

I still laugh when I look back on some of my old scribblings. When I started practicing automatic writing years ago, I used to write down the strangest things. Writing sessions would often start at around three o'clock in the morning, after I had woken up from a dream or gone to the bathroom. As I was drifting back off to sleep one of my ears would start ringing, sometimes so loudly I couldn't ignore it.

I soon learned that if I picked up my pen and paper and started writing, the ringing noise would go away. Back in those days, I had an enormous bedroom and had built a pyramid of copper piping at one end of the room out. At the time, I believed that sitting under the pyramid shaped frame helped me to be more receptive to incoming information, but when winter came, I decided I would just have to practice my automatic writing from the cosy warmth of my bed.

The words that flowed from my pen at that time made little sense, if any. Here again I would like to remind you of the rusty pipe analogy. Much of what I wrote was the same sentence or idea repeated over and over again, nonsensical babbling I could easily have ignored as rubbish. It would have been easy to forget the whole thing.

I also received a great deal of "information" in garbled French and Elizabethan-style English, complete with "thees," "thys," and "thous"! Odd as this all seemed to me at the time, it didn't feel like a problem. I knew that my Guidance was contacting me at that early hour because that was when my mind was least cluttered with the thoughts and concerns of my waking life. It was the easiest time for my Guides to get through to me, when the activity of my conscious mind was at its lowest ebb.

It is a peculiar feeling at first, this business of automatic writing. We are so accustomed to our minds supposedly being in control of everything we do. Letting go and allowing something to flow through you and onto the page can be a challenge.

I believe automatic writing has been around for a very long time; writers of poetry, prose, and music throughout the ages speak of urgent inspiration that simply can't be ignored and must be written down immediately without any censorship.

Some of our greatest inventors and scientists have had similar experiences. Dr. Samuel Hahnemann, the man who invented modern homoeopathy was known to work and write throughout the night, as if driven by a force more powerful than himself, often not sleeping for two days and nights in a row. He did this for many years, well into old age.

Many of history's great composers—not only Mozart—are renowned for how incredibly young they were when they composed their miraculous music, and for how quickly they wrote them.

Automatic writing is often a very quick process that doesn't allow the conscious mind time to analyse or criticise what is being written. You become a Channel for a stream of Divine Inspiration that completely bypasses your own knowledge base and thinking mind. You can always go back and correct what you've written later if you like, but once your rusty water becomes a clear flow, you probably won't need to.

When I was young, I used to quite enjoy writing poetry, but the most beautiful poems I have ever written came to me decades later, at three or four in the morning. They took less than five minutes to write and needed no correction of any kind. Here is one example:

The World Within

She floats on mists of sand and sea
'Tween day and starry night,
Longing only to be free
Her sovereign, holy right.
The gold and silver of the dawn
Flows gently through her hair,
And such a scene of beauty born
Great things beyond compare.
Her heav'nly heart and earthly mind
Now shining with the Light,
With joy of life of different kind
Comes seeking from the night.
A prison in her heart once was
But dwells in there no more,
This freedom that she longs for has
Come rolling to her shore.
Finally after all these years
Her arms can now embrace,
Whilst letting go of all Life's tears
The beauty of this place.
Perfection, neither here nor there
Resides the world within,
All that is good and fine and rare
Exists inside her skin.

So inward now the journey goes
A vast place to explore,
Into the world where heart-felt knows
The shining, open door.

—BELINDAGRACE AND FRIENDS 1–7–2003

You may have noticed that I signed this poem "BelindaGrace and Friends"—I do this because I know it wasn't myself alone who wrote it. I take the credit for developing my ability to write automatically to such a beautiful degree, for making myself available so to speak, but the actual content came from something greater than my conscious mind.

I call it the Universe, God/Goddess/All That Is, or my Angels, Spirit Guides, or Divine Guidance. It was inspiration (to be filled with Spirit/God) pure and simple, not something my conscious mind had been working on. I had help of the most wonderful kind in writing it and I like to acknowledge that.

This poem, like the others I've written, came to me unexpectedly at what could be considered an inconvenient hour. It's wonderful to have these spontaneous bursts of creativity, but it is only one of the many forms of automatic writing.

The form that my students, clients, and I use most frequently is automatic writing on demand, an amazingly useful tool that can help you receive meaningful answers to your problems, be more creative, or even write a book. In the following exercise, you will find out how to get started—beyond that are as many ways to use automatic writing as you can imagine.

Naturally, I recommend working with all the techniques in the previous chapters of this book beforehand, as it is much easier to receive clear information with a Channel that has already been set up for that purpose. It took me about four years to develop past the gobbledeygook stages of my early scribblings to the clarity of the poem you have just read. I believe one of the reasons it took me so long was that I was just muddling through it on my own.

Nowadays my students start practicing automatic writing in the fourth week of the courses I teach, often with stunning results, because their Channels have been reactivated and strengthened, and they have learned how to connect to their Divine Guidance at will. If you have been using this book as instructed, you will have learned how to do this too and are now building on those important foundations.

Automatic writing is not about writing down what it is that you want to hear and then pretending you channelled it from a higher source; it is a genuine tool that allows you to access information from beyond the limited realm of human thinking, free of all the usual manipulations and underlying motives that come with most of our opinions and desires. So before starting the following exercise, give some thought to the kinds of questions you would like to ask.

It is always advisable to start with questions that don't hold a big emotional charge for you personally. For example if you ask a question such as "Am I going to lose my job?" or "Is my boyfriend going to ask me to marry him?" it is very difficult to remain impartial. Until you have a reasonable mastery of this tool, it's best to steer clear of these kinds of enquiries because your impartiality is very important.

All the processes in this book are tools to help us surrender and allow ourselves to be guided by something greater than what we think we are.

The following list of questions will give you an idea of the kind of questions that are useful when just starting out. Many of these are questions I use in my classes.

- What is the meaning and/or purpose of rainbows?
- Is there life on other planets?
- What is the purpose of human suffering?
- What purpose does an individual such as Adolf Hitler serve in the process of human development?
- What do I need to do or not do; understand/realise/ embrace/let go of in order to live a happier and more fulfilling life?

Try to notice the different feelings you have when Channelling an answer for a question you know absolutely nothing about, compared to one where you already have some opinions or beliefs. This will be a useful indicator for you as to what feels like an impartial Channel and what doesn't.

These are just a small sample of the questions you can start with. Choose one and follow the steps of the exercise below to start your automatic writing practice.

Allow your hand and pen do the writing for you without intervention from your mind. Remember, there are no right or wrong answers. Be aware of your intention to be impartial and let the information flow.

EXERCISE TEN

AUTOMATIC WRITING—JUST DO IT!

Requirements: A quiet location where you can sit and write comfortably
Notebook or journal
Pen or pencil

Time required: 10–30 minutes (more than half an hour will give you writer's cramp!)

- Make yourself comfortable and remember to connect to the beam of white light that flows down through you from the Universe and into the core of the Earth, and the beam of red light that flows up to you from the Earth's core and up out through the top of your head.

- Sit with that energy flow for a moment until you feel "plugged in" or connected. Note: Eventually this connection will become instantaneous, activated by your intention to work with this, or one of the other techniques.

- Focus your intent on automatic writing and allowing yourself to become a channel for information that you will write down.

- Let your conscious, thinking mind take a step back. Do your best to accept that the information you are about to write down may not have anything to do with what you think, believe, or have learned. Let this be a relaxing process, remaining calm and alert while letting whatever information that wants to come to you flow.

- Take up your pen and notebook, and focus on one question for a moment, all the while remaining aware of your intention. Write the chosen question at the top of the page first to help you get started. Note: When you are new to this practice, it is common to feel stuck or blocked at first, so be patient with yourself. Sometimes it's helpful to choose another question or to word it in a way that is more acceptable to you.

- Let your hand do the writing; let the words flow out onto the page however they come. This exercise is not a test and you aren't expected to come up with eloquent or flowery verses at this early stage. Let it all happen without judgement or criticism, and please don't try to read it as you are writing—doing so will certainly tempt you to analyse your writing and will block the flow.

- The only time to stop and read is when you feel you're completely finished with the question. If you would like to attempt more thaagn one question on your first sitting, go right ahead; notice the differences in the quality of the responses.

- Practice, practice, practice whenever you can! Asking friends, friends of friends, and family to give you simple questions can be helpful too, some of a more general nature, and eventually ones that are of a personal nature as well.

- Be sure to read your responses carefully and reflect on what they might be trying to tell you in addition to the literal meanings. Some of you may get incomprehensible or nonsensical stuff like I did at first; others will get single words that make individual points rather than forming a sentence. At other times, you may get a more steady flow only to find that it stops abruptly for no apparent reason. Just go with it and allow your skill to develop in its own natural way. Keep practicing and expanding your repertoire. Once you have more confidence with this skill, you can try answering questions that have an emotional charge. Asking these kinds of questions will develop your ability to be impartial and make you into a more effective Channel. The more you are able to keep your own ideas and opinions out of your receptivity, the more space you will leave for the Universe to work its magic. It is also possible to use Automatic Writing as a way to get information and guidance for a friend, family member, or client. However, when you are channelling information for another person, responsibilities exist on both sides.

As a clairvoyant, it is very important to make the other person aware of your level of experience, or lack thereof. Your other key responsibility is to hold an intention of wanting only the best for the other person by being the clearest channel possible. This means being honest with yourself about whether or not your own opinions or judgements are colouring the information you are bringing through.

Be humble and let them know that perhaps some of your own ideas are in the mix of your channelled information.

The other responsibility lies with the receiver. The exact same piece of information will often be understood in ten different ways by ten different people as they filter it through their own experiences and beliefs. Be clear with those on the receiving end that how they interpret the information they are given, and how they choose to act upon it, is up to them and totally their own responsibility.

Personally, when I first practiced in this way, I found it was best to know as little about the person as possible, so I preferred working with friends of friends, rather than my own. As I became more experienced I was able to channel impartial information for those familiar to me as well.

But no matter what your level of experience or who you are channelling for, it is possible to channel some wonderful information and creative work. Here is an example of some of the magical work that my students have achieved. Heather was a participant in one of my nine-week courses; she is a scientist and had never done any work of this nature before. This is what she wrote in response to the question "How can we connect more to the energies of the Goddess and bring more of the Goddess into our lives?"

The Goddess Within

You are all the Goddess. Connect with yourselves, your own inner beauty and love. You are beautiful within and it should shine for all to see.

Trust in yourselves and know that you are all very special and beautiful people.

Love your life, your love and your inner self and laugh, laugh, laugh and be happy!

You are as special as everyone on this planet and you should show your inner Goddess to the world.

Your beauty, kindness and natural ways are so very special and should be shared and celebrated to everyone.

Know that you are all very beautiful and your love will shine through.

Be kind to yourselves and know that all is well.

For this is all you deserve and more.

Take care special ones for you are worthy of all and more.

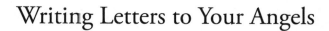

CHAPTER EIGHT

Writing Letters to Your Angels

While we're in a writing mood, you may like to know that one the easiest and most effective ways to communicate with your Angels is to write them a letter. Putting things down on paper is a marvellous way to focus your energy and attention.

When you first meet your Angels and Spirit Guides, it can be difficult to know how to stay in contact with them or to communicate with them about something specific or profound.

In the chapter on meeting your Angels and Spirit Guides I recommended that you speak to them in your mind or even out loud, and you should definitely do this on a daily basis to help your relationship with them grow. So when you wake up in the morning, ask your Angels and Spirit Guides to gather around you and join you for the day.

However when it comes to something very specific or important to you, it might be worth taking the time to write it down. There is an energy or power in writing that goes beyond the thoughts that move around in your head.

Writing sharpens the focus of those ideas and increases the intensity by turning something nonphysical (thoughts) into something physical (the written word).

If you have a problem that continues to bother you, the actual process of writing the letter can help you recognise some possible solutions even before you have sent it.

The best time to write a letter to your Angels or Spirit Guides is when you get a strong urge to do so; that is when you will put the greatest emotion and intensity into it.

Don't feel that you have to hold back or be excessively polite either; you cannot offend your Angels or Spirit Guides, they've literally seen it all before. Instead, be genuine about your desire for a solution or the item or situation you want.

Sometimes we believe our prayers or requests go unanswered, but the truth is we only get what we *really* want. Even if we have convinced ourselves that we want a certain thing at the level of the logical mind, we will not receive it if it is clear that our hearts yearn for something else. Remember, the Universe doesn't speak any particular language, it responds to our feelings about life and ourselves.

My clients, students, and I have had some delightful and interesting responses to our letters over the years. One recent example was really quite amazing. Charlotte was a student of mine and had a very important job in an insurance firm. With all her knowledge and experience it should have been a rewarding and even enjoyable role, but her time with the company was fraught with difficulties from day one. Her biggest problem was the total lack of respect with which some of her junior staff treated her. They spoke to her rudely and a couple of them even openly defied her and refused to do as she directed even though they were fully aware that she was their supervisor.

After three months of this Charlotte went home one evening after work feeling completely exasperated. Frustrated and angry about what was going on, she wrote a very passionate letter to her Angels. She addressed it to them by name and didn't hold back on her true feelings about these people, their rudeness, and her own hurt, embarrassment, and confusion. All her years of training and experience in this field had not prepared her for such insubordination, and she had no idea what to do. Everything came pouring out onto the page; itself a cathartic process.

When she asked her Angels how to send this letter to them, she was answered by a strong feeling to take the letter out into the yard and burn it. She also asked them to give her a sign that they had received the letter. By this time it was late, so she burned the letter just outside the door before going inside to sleep.

The next day, Charlotte left for work and as she opened the gate, she noticed a large feather stuck on the top of it. This had never happened before; she felt very strongly that it was the sign from her Angels to signify the receipt of her letter.

Once at work, the following few hours proved to be amazing, as each of the four people who had been so uncooperative up to this time made contact with her by email or phone. One of them phoned her and actually apologised for his behaviour, another called and asked her advice on a certain project and listened attentively to her advice. The other two people were suddenly friendly and professional in their approach.

Charlotte was stunned at the transformations; she had not spoken to any of them directly—the only thing that had changed since the day before was that she had written the letter to her Angels. Now all the people involved were being nice to her.

At this point, you could be forgiven for thinking that this is the end of the story, but a few days later two more feathers crossed her path in very unusual places. She had a distinct feeling that something major was going to happen later that day. She didn't know what it was going to be, but felt that the feathers were her Angels' way of letting her know they were near and that everything would be okay.

At lunchtime, she was summoned to the top floor to see her manager. The meeting wasn't scheduled, and they would not tell her what it was about over the phone. Once she got to her manager's office, he promptly sat her down and told her that her employment contract was being terminated. Her probationary period had a few days to run and there was nothing she could do or say—it was over. She left the company that day for good.

Naturally Charlotte was upset at first, and felt that she had been unfairly treated; then it dawned on her what was really going on. When she was totally honest with herself, she had to admit that she hadn't liked the job from the first day, and that the only thing that had kept her there was a fear of change and the loss of her good salary. She didn't think it would look good on her CV to leave the job too soon and chose to stick with the "rational" path of putting up with it.

However, Charlotte had triggered a big energy shift by writing that letter. Not only did the Angels show her that they could help with the superficial problem of the difficult people, they also responded to the true desire expressed by her which was "I hate my job but I cannot logically justify leaving it at this time. Help!" In losing her job, Charlotte actually got what she really wanted.

We all try to talk ourselves into doing what seems right or safe; most people do it for their entire lives, seeing anything else as an unjustifiable risk and fearing the criticism of others. Charlotte's Angels helped her to see the bigger picture of what was really going on in her life and acknowledge that she had been longing for a career change for years. Suddenly her situation changed, and instead of fearing life without her job she realised how many other opportunities she had. So caught up in the idea that she had to be self-sufficient, she hadn't even realised that her husband was willing to support her while she explored new career and study options. Sure, they would have to watch their spending for a while, but they would get by, and everything would be alright. The Universe responded to her true desire and she was catapulted into the next phase of her life.

Charlotte's story illustrates just one of the ways in which your help will come. Often our minds are quite fixed on the way things "should" happen and we miss the gifts that come our way because they don't look like we expected them to. The nasty, uncooperative people whom Charlotte had to supervise were actually the Universe's way of telling her that she no longer belonged in that kind of environment. When she didn't take the hint and cried for help, that good old cosmic boot came along to give her a nudge in a much healthier direction.

This is powerful stuff we are working with here; it transforms people's lives every day. So be honest with yourself about what you *really* want and be prepared for it to come to you in unusual ways. Charlotte could have wallowed in the idea of her termination as a disaster, remaining angry and hurt for any length of time. What she decided to do instead was to see it as a gift and the chance to start a whole new career path. I was happy to learn that a few weeks after her big life change, her husband received a huge pay rise. Charlotte never once looked back, and doesn't miss her old corporate life whatsoever.

EXERCISE ELEVEN

WRITING A LETTER TO YOUR ANGELS
OR SPIRIT GUIDES

Requirements: A quiet location where you can sit and
write comfortably
Writing paper
Envelope
Pen or pencil

Optional: Candles
Music
Oil burner with some nice essential oil of your choice
Postage stamps

Time required: 10–30 minutes

- Start by tuning yourself in to the energy flow through your Channel to create your connection to your Divine Guidance and ask your Angels and Spirit Guides to gather around you.

- If you like, set a nice mood by lighting a candle and playing some relaxing music.

- Be as clear as you can about what it is you want and write it all down on your writing paper.

- If you don't know the names of your Angels and Spirit Guides yet then simply address it to "My Dear Angels" or something similar.

- Write the letter as you would to a friend who knows you very well and wants to help you. Your Angels and Spirit Guides are not hung up on formalities, so make it as friendly and direct as you want. Note: Don't leave anything out because of some mistaken belief that you can overload them or ask too much. Your celestial friends can deal with anything you can dish out.

- Once you have finished writing, put your letter in an envelope and address it to them. You can even put a stamp on it to make it feel more authentic!

- Ask your Angels or Spirit Guides how they would like you to send it and go with the first impulse that comes to you, whether it be burying it, burning it, casting it out onto the ocean, tearing it up into tiny pieces, putting it in a drawer or even in the recycling. I have put some of my letters in the post.

- As you "send" your letter ask your Angels or Guides for a sign to let you know it has been received.

- Once you have completed and sent the letter do not dwell on the situation or the possible solution, trust that all that can be done is being done by your Angels and wait for the results to manifest for you without anxiety.

The signs that your letter has been received by your friends are as varied as they are. Some of you might notice a feather in an unusual place, or the words of a song you have heard a hundred times may suddenly strike you as important.

When I ask for a sign of acknowledgement, I am often shown a rainbow in the most peculiar of places, maybe one in the sky when there hasn't been any rain, in the colours of someone's clothing, or a rainbow lorikeet perching on my window sill.

The signs are often very subtle and you may miss them at first. If you send a message to your Angels and/or Spirit Guides with your strong and clear intention, you can be sure it has been received. Being given a sign is really just a reassurance for the mind. Once you have sent the letter your only job is to let go of the problem and let the solutions come by being open to them appearing in ways you had not anticipated. This is not the Universe trying to test you; it is just trying to give you the best possible result and usually one that will exceed your expectations.

Most of all this process should be done in a spirit of fun. Even when your problems are serious or your situation is dire your Angels and Spirit Guides will often bring a solution to you that is humorous or lighthearted; this is not flippancy but rather an acknowledgement that we can achieve a lot more when we are joyous and relaxed as opposed to squeezing the life force out of it with grim determination.

Write your letter, send it, and then relax. You will be prompted to take the next step when it is required.

The only thing you need to practice with this technique is your ability to recognise and respond to the prompts and signs. This ability will develop with practice, so write lots of letters in order to give yourself plenty of opportunities to improve.

A few years ago I had a response from my Angels that took my breath away. It was the middle of winter and I had a very strong urge to write a letter to my Angels, so I sat down and wrote with great passion and detail.

When I was finished they told me very clearly to go and cast my letter out onto the ocean. I live minutes from the beach so this was easy enough, but they were very specific as they told me it had to be on the next high tide which was at ten o'clock that night!

The wind and waves were wild that evening as it had been stormy for days, but I rugged up and went out as instructed. After two attempts at flinging my envelope out into the crashing waves I was becoming cold, wet, and a little exasperated. I told myself that if the third throw was no good I was going to take my letter and go home. The third attempt was good of course, and my letter got sucked out into the night.

The following day I tried to go for a walk on the beach three or four times but every time I went to walk out of the building the rain lashed down and I went back inside. Finally at around three o'clock it looked fine enough to go out. The tide was very low and the expanse of flat, glassy sand shone in the wintry sun. As I passed the spot on the beach where I had stood the night before, I began to wonder if I was going to get a sign.

As I continued to walk I noticed some writing in the sand a couple of hundred metres further along. Tourists and children were always writing messages in the sand, usually along the lines of "Johnny loves Jane" or "I was here" and things like that. The first noticeably different things about this message was that it was very long and written so neatly it was as though it had been meticulously measured out, the lettering also looked very fresh, as though they had only just been written but there was no one nearby. It was the words however, that both stunned me and made me laugh; they read:

> "Wednesday 10th of May. We hope you
> have had a nice day. We look forward to read-
> ing your letter."

After reading that message in the sand there was certainly no doubt that my Angels had received my letter.

CHAPTER NINE

Breaking the Cycle—Releasing Your Past-Life Patterns

The phrase "You can't take it with you" is only partially right. You may not be able to take your favourite shoes or your bank balance with you when you pass over, but unresolved emotional issues will stay with you until you deal with them. Your soul will keep attracting the same kinds of people and circumstances to you, life after life after life, until you get it. This may seem cruel to some but it is just the working of a very orderly Universe which demonstrates that every action—be it a feeling, belief, thought, word, or deed (yes, all of those things are actions)—has an effect.

By examining your past lives and resolving the negative patterns or issues that you still carry from those times, you can create positive changes in your current life. Hearing about a past life may be a curiosity or entertainment for some, but for me and my clients it has become a path to greater understanding of the self and the freedom that brings. So it's not about dwelling on the past at all—it's about making the present more pleasant.

In the winter of 1998 a young woman came to see me for a reading. She was on crutches, with her right foot heavily bandaged. I soon discovered that she was only twenty-four, and that, despite all kinds of examinations by specialists, including x-rays, no cause for her problem had been found. Finally, in an attempt to give it some sort of label, she had been diagnosed with gout, which seemed quite unlikely given her youth and healthy lifestyle. She was in excruciating pain—moving or touching the foot was impossible, but she did not want to take the steroids she had been prescribed.

This was the first time I had been asked to work on someone with acute physical pain, but I did what I always do: I closed my eyes and waited for the guidance and information to come.

What followed in the reading was the tale of Claudia, a detailed description of one of my young client's past lives where she was a foreign gypsy girl with a flair for herbal medicine.

CLAUDIA'S STORY REVEALED

France, 17th Century

It would be fair to say that Claudia was an enigma to most of the folk in her large French town. She was a strange looking creature to most people's eyes for she had the pale skin of someone from the north, and the thick, dark, wavy hair of a Mediterranean woman. Her appearance was somewhat unkempt, and her dress sense would often cause the people she met to believe that she was a gypsy.

Some of the town's people liked her, some were curious, but most found her distasteful and avoided her.

However, Claudia had great skill with medicinal herbs and some townsfolk sought her out as a last resort, exasperated by the lack of results from their physicians or the inability to afford one. Although people were often grateful for her vast and eclectic body of knowledge, most still found it prudent not to acknowledge her openly in public.

Claudia was not concerned with her herbal healing arts on this particular night however, because the person she was going to visit was already beyond her kind of help. He was a boy who had died at the age of fifteen after being flogged by his master for theft. The master would not allow the boy to have any medical attention, and when the boy died, the master had him cheaply and hastily buried in the town cemetery. No one else attended the and no one seemed to care, except Claudia.

Now, having waited until late and all was quiet, she crept into the cemetery in order to sing some prayers over the fresh grave and place some petals and herbs upon it, to help hasten and ease the passage of the young man's soul.

As she sang and spoke to him, and placed some flower petals and other simple items in a particular pattern on the earth, she heard voices coming closer through the darkness. She hoped that they would pass, but it seemed they were coming directly into the cemetery.

The last thing she wanted was to be discovered there by people who were already somewhat suspicious of her behaviour. She didn't want to be imprisoned or ejected from the town, as had happened to other misfits in the past.

Claudia knew there was only one entrance to the grounds—it lead towards the voices. Unwilling to risk being caught, she ran instead towards the perimeter fence and began to scramble over it.

The fence was a tall, wrought iron affair with large spikes along the top. It was dangerous to climb but she wasn't thinking clearly and just wanted to get out. She pulled herself to the top and brought her right foot over, lost her balance momentarily and impaled her right foot on one of the huge spikes. Frantic now, Claudia managed to pull her foot back up off the spike and scramble down the other side of the fence.

Claudia did not dare to go out into the streets for several days, and felt fortunate that she could at least tend to her wound properly.

A week later, hunger forced her to go out to the market for food, but no one paid her any mind. Her life soon returned to normal, and she was never questioned about her whereabouts that night. She listened for gossip on the street but heard none.

Claudia remained in that town for many years, helping those who came to her with ailments and still performing the occasional ceremony over the graves of the forgotten people of the town. It was her fate also to remain an unsung member of her community, despite helping so many for little or even no remuneration.

At the end of her life, she was given a pauper's burial and was forgotten. Most would have described her life as unimportant, but Claudia felt differently. She had enjoyed her work, freedom, and independence so much that even though she was nearly seventy when she died, she felt she wanted to continue to be here in the world. People needed her and here is where she wanted to stay. So her soul remained connected to the Earth plane.

After the reading, my client told me she was a Naturopathy student and dreamed of having her own practice one day as a healer. She loved learning about all the remedies and herbs, and we could see from her life as Claudia that she was already well prepared for this kind of career path.

A week later she came back to see me, walking very well without her crutches, but the pain in her foot was not entirely gone. We did a bit more clearing work and asked her Angels to make sure that aspect of her soul had gone completely to the Light. As always, everything that needed to be done was taken care of, and all her attachment to that past life was released. The pain in her foot cleared up completely within the next week and has never troubled her again.

The above is a graphic illustration of how the energy from an unresolved past life can come back to affect us in the present; and just one example of the good things that can happen for us when we learn how to liberate ourselves from our pasts.

Some of the experiences you had in your previous incarnations still play a part in the way you feel and behave today. When you came into this current lifetime, your soul decided to have certain types of experiences for many different reasons. All of them will ultimately lead to greater spiritual growth and awareness, something we sometimes refer to as enlightenment. Such a phenomenon broadly separates into three large categories: experiences, people, and of course, past-life issues.

New experiences, such as living in a country that you never have before, or doing anything that you have not yet done in a previous life, are designed to help you to expand your sense of who you are.

Then there are the experiences similar to the things you enjoyed or were good at in the past and want more time to refine. You may be drawn to a certain hobby or vocation with a power that you can't explain, perhaps even finding that you are a "natural" at this activity.

It is equally possible to be drawn to certain people with whom you immediately feel a positive bond—instinctively you feel that you have been friends before, but in the absence of "proof" most people let that notion go.

The third category, past-life issues, is much less pleasant. This consists of all the experiences which bring you reminders of the feelings, beliefs, thoughts, words, and actions that caused you some kind of pain, misfortune, or confusion in your past life or lives. The category will also encompass all the traits about yourself that you don't like, your negative beliefs and expectations, and the things you wouldn't or seemingly couldn't deal with and resolve at an earlier time.

Even after living hundreds of lives, there are still many new and pleasant experiences available, but most of us will also have a closet full of baggage dragging us down.

Most of the lives that will be shown to you are the ones that hold something you have not yet understood or come to terms with, and only you can know what those things are. You are the only person qualified to interpret the meaning of what you are shown.

When a person comes to me for a reading, I usually ask them only for the most mundane of information: name, date of birth, address, and phone numbers. Yet after the reading they report to me how amazed they are by the similarities between the past life that came up to be cleared and what they are currently experiencing.

Most of us have had hundreds of lives here on Earth, some of which may have only lasted a few minutes or hours, as infant mortality was extremely high in bygone centuries. No matter how brief, every life still counts; and although it may seem tragic to those who are left behind, the soul of each human being knows exactly when the time is right to depart.

The Angels have always told me and my clients that there's no such thing as an untimely, premature, or accidental death; each soul has a contract to incarnate here on Earth for specific reasons, experiences, and periods of time. This is not a haphazard Universe; everything happens for a reason even if we find it difficult to accept. Your soul will remain in this incarnation for exactly the amount of time that it needs to in order to experience what it came here for.

Once you reach the point where you have lived many lives and have connected with some of your memories of them, you'll begin to have compassion for and understanding of people from other cultures and walks of life. At the same time, you'll realise that you too have walked in many different kinds of shoes.

Many of my clients are amazed to find that they have been both victim and villain in the great story of humanity. We all love to hear stories of how hard we tried, how good we were, and how unfairly we were treated; but it is also very humbling to know that at some point we were all criminals, liars, cheats, and even murderers.

Those of you who are women in this life have lived here before as men, and vice versa, so it does no good to point fingers anymore and try to blame other groups or genders for the "mess" we are in. We have all been greedy and we have all been generous, a fact that is vital to understand if the wounds of humanity are ever to be fully healed. Discovering that you have been many different kinds of people in the past is a process of self-forgiveness and an act of courage. None of us are superior to another.

The past-life reading and healing process my Angels taught me is very thorough. It's a process that goes much deeper than just telling a story. Over the years, I have had many people come to me and tell me that another reader had told them they had a past life in a certain place, doing this or that. A snippet of the story was thrown their way but nothing more. No detail about the experiences of that life, the lessons that went unlearned or whether or not there were unresolved issues remaining.

In our process you will be able to discover not only as much detail about your past-life story as you can, you will also be taught how to resolve the issues from that life and move on. It is a complete process that will leave you with a greater understanding of who you are and the journey you are on.

If you keep making the same mistakes, coming up against similar obstacles and frustrations, find yourself dealing with the same kind of difficult people over and over again, clearing past-life patterns may help you.

Whether a hurt went unaddressed a week ago, a year ago, a lifetime ago, or centuries ago is of no consequence—the fact remains that it still needs to be healed. Past-life review and release will help you clear these kind

of pains and the patterns and problems they cause forever.

EXERCISE TWELVE

PAST-LIFE RELEASE

In this simple step-by-step exercise, you will review and
release one of your own past lives. Please fully read the
guidelines a couple of times before doing the exercise.
At first glance you may think there is a lot to remember,
but it really is very simple and has a logical, step-by-step
flow.

Requirements: A quiet location where you can lie or sit
   comfortably
   Pen
   Notebook or journal

Time required: Approximately 30 minutes

- Have a pen and notepad or journal within arm's
  reach of where you will sit.
- Make yourself comfortable, close your eyes, and ask
  your Angels and Spirit Guides to come and gather
  closely around you. Tune in to your intention to
  review and release one of your own past lives. If you
  are feeling particularly troubled by a certain issue at
  this time, you may want to ask your Angels and Spirit
  Guides to help you see the past life in which the root

cause of that issue was created; or you may be happy to go with the flow and review whatever life comes up.

- Imagine all the colours of the rainbow—red, orange, yellow, green, blue, indigo, and violet—picture those colours on your Inner Screen. Contemplate them for a minute or so, and allow yourself to be drawn into one of those colours.

- Allow yourself to be drawn in deeply, as though the colour is engulfing you or you are diving into it; gently reminding yourself of your intention to revisit one of your own past lives. You may feel as though you are travelling through a tunnel of this colour, or imagine you are swimming or floating through it. Take as long as you like on this colourful journey, there is no rush.

- Gently direct yourself to emerge from the colour into the environment of your past life. Give yourself time to get a sense of having arrived. Start by focusing on your feet or some other part of your body or appearance, such as clothing. Allow the story to unfold on your Inner Screen in your mind's eye. Don't strain yourself to see anything, just let it happen. Allow your mind to go blank so that your past-life story can come to you, like the return of a very old memory.

- The story may come to you fleetingly, as a feeling or as unconnected images or sounds. Stay with it, relax, and don't try to analyse or understand anything yet.

In your mind, ask questions about the things you would like to know, such as whether you were male or female. What country are you in? What century or year is it? What sort of family did you have? What did you do with your time? Did you get an education, work, or get married?

- Try to imagine you're watching a movie of your past life playing in your head; you have the remote control, so rewind it to the beginning and press "Play" to begin chronologically.

- Stay with the experience until you feel you've been shown everything that you were meant to see; coax as much detail out of it as you can and continue to nudge the information along until you sense that you are coming to the end of that life story. Most people are curious to know how old they were when they died and what they died from, so ask about these things if they interest you.

- Before you leave, ask why you were shown this particular past life and why it is still not fully resolved; why did this aspect of your soul not go to the Light? Note: There could be many reasons, including deeply held religious beliefs in that life, loved ones you didn't want to be separated from, or a desire you were never able to realise.

- When you've done your best to get a sense of answers to these questions, call your Angels and Spirit Guides in to assist that aspect of yourself on its journey up to the Light. Imagine all the heaviness and unhappiness from that lifetime being absorbed by the Light; that part of your soul being compassionately embraced and welcomed without question, and experience the relief that comes.

- The next step is simply to let all the beautiful, positive energy, memories, and personality traits from that life be returned to you in full. Picture a stream of golden energy flowing back down to you, pouring into your heart, returning to you all that was good and desirable from that life. All these qualities will be reintegrated into your being in a way that is compatible and useful for you in this lifetime.

- Then, when you are ready, you can begin the return trip to your present place and time. Use the same colour that helped to transport you to the past life. (If your colour changes, that's also perfectly fine.) Moving back along through your colourful superhighway, you have a calm sense of knowing that you are returning to your present life. Imagine yourself homing in on the country you live in, then the state, then the city, then the street, then the building, and so on, all the way back to the room you are in and the chair you are sitting on.

- Take a moment or two, eyes still closed, to become fully aware of your physical body again. Breathe deeply, feel the weight of your body in the chair, wriggle your fingers and toes, and have a stretch if you like.

Say your name out loud, for example "I am Belinda," then open you eyes.

- Before doing anything else, take up your pen and paper and write down everything you can remember about your experience. It is very important to do this right away because your memory of this journey can fade, just like the memory of a dream. Jot down details including any feelings or emotions you had during the review.

- This final step is very important. It's the step where tell you—"Don't worry! There is no wrong way to do this, you did it your way, and you did it well. You read the guidelines, you let it happen, and that is always the best way." The *most* important step in all of these techniques is your intention—everything else will be done for you by your Angels and Spirit Guides whether you see it or not.

A Past Life Revealed

We have all had many positive and beautiful experiences in our pasts, however these nice memories are not usually the ones we need to come to terms with and resolve. The happy memories are much more easily accepted and integrated, whereas the hurts and pains of everyday life are not. I believe that one of the main reasons that our painful experiences go unresolved is because deep down we always blame ourselves.

Even if we are outwardly blaming others for our problems, inside a little voice is saying "What's wrong with me? Why is this happening to me? Why can't I get it right?" It is the lack of forgiveness that we afford ourselves that stops us from going to the Light. We feel undeserving of the unconditional love that is offered to us at the end of each incarnation so we hold on to the negative feelings, hoping they will just disappear with time. One of the key causes of depression that I have come across is a past-life experience that was so traumatic for the individual that they lost their will to live. These traumatic experiences can range from the downright harrowing to a mild shock or fright; it all depends on the individual and the effect it had on him or her at the time.

One young woman who came to see me seemed to have everything to live for. She did her best to appear cheerful and positive while she was around other people, but by herself at home it was a very different story.

She felt suicidal and cried herself to sleep almost every night. She had kept these low feelings mostly to herself because she found that when she tried to talk to people about how badly she felt, they seemed unable to understand or take her seriously. All they saw was a pretty, successful, and likeable young woman with a good job and a loving fiancé. They couldn't really relate to the fact that inside she was miserable. She didn't understand it either and she felt foolish, almost disbelieving her own feelings because she always felt better around other people.

Her fiancé had spoken to her about setting a wedding date; they were to marry six months from her first visit with me. They did not yet live together and she was dreading the whole thing because she knew she would not be able to repress her sad and frightened feelings every night after they were married. This lovely lady had not told her fiancé about her "problem" and the counselling she'd undergone had not been able to uncover the source of her seemingly inexplicable unhappiness.

We commenced the reading as always and I was shown a past life of hers which would be enough to turn anyone's hair grey.

During a lifetime in London in the early to mid-1800s she had been stalked and eventually kidnapped by a mentally deranged uncle. Her family were working class and she received a basic education, able only to read and write a little. They lived in the north east of London in the area of Finchley. In order to help the family supplement its income, at the age of twelve she went to work two or three days a week as a kind of trainee governess or nanny. It was a large household, the man of the house a very successful barrister with a sickly wife and six children. There was plenty of work to do and she enjoyed it, walking to and from her employer's home at the same time each day.

Meanwhile, her father's brother was being welcomed back into the family fold after a falling out many years earlier. She had not really had a chance to get to know him as he had been absent from the family since she was four or five.

During the reading, it was unclear what the problem had been between her uncle and her father, but there was a strong sense that he had been in prison for some time for reasons no one seemed inclined to discuss.

Relations with her uncle and her family were on the mend and everyone seemed happy enough. She continued to go to work at the barrister's home and was soon offered full time employment there, much to the joy of everyone.

Her uncle, who now visited the family fairly often, would come and meet her in the evenings outside her employer's front gate, and walk her home. She understood he was trying to be friendly, but there was something about him that made her feel uncomfortable. His behaviour towards her became overly familiar; he encroached on her physical space, touching her hair and being somewhat possessive of her when other people were around. He became angry when she hinted that she would rather walk home on her own, and he would sometimes insist that they walk a much longer distance than necessary to get back to her family.

One night, when his behaviour was quite unreasonable, she tried to run away from him. He had demanded that they walk through a large park together. It was cold, nearly dark, and she felt afraid. She fled, but he caught up with her easily and, even though she struggled, he dragged her across the park and into a dilapidated building. It turned out to be a kind of squat very near to the grimy bed-sit where her uncle lived.

He tied her up and kept her there for days, even joining in the frantic search for her with her distraught family, saying that she had not been waiting as usual when he had gone to collect her the previous day.

On the seventh day of her ordeal she died of dehydration: terrified, alone, and only a few miles from where she lived. Her uncle had been very clever, living in a small bed-sit just a block or two away, but spending most of his time at the squat, so when the police searched his home—the bed-sit— they found no sign of his niece. He buried her beneath the floorboards and her body was never found.

The reasons for this man's behaviour and mental state are too complicated to go into here. However it was clear to us that the trauma of this experience had frightened her so much that she had lost her will to live. That aspect of her soul did not go to the Light when she died because she was so terrified and disorientated and wanted only to return to her parents.

Once we had heard the whole story, her Angels came and helped that aspect of her soul go to the Light to find peace once and for all. When an aspect of your soul that has been in limbo since the end of a particular life finally goes to the Light, miraculous things happen.

All the heaviness and negativity from that lifetime are allowed to fall away; any negative emotions or memories connected with that life are absorbed into the Light and embraced in a compassionate way.

This is a deeply healing process because a part of you that has been frightened and in pain for a long time is finally going home and experiencing the all-encompassing and unconditional love of the Creator. All positive memories, qualities, and feelings from that lifetime are then returned to you and reintegrated into your awareness in a way that is useful for you in this lifetime. You are reunited with a part of yourself that has always been there but was disconnected from you until now.

The changes in this young woman's life were remarkable. She became her true self again; happy, positive, and calm. She began to look forward to her wedding and the life she and her fiancé would build. The fears that had plagued her seemed to evaporate and the feelings of confusion and desperation went away. Now, years later, she is happily married and expecting her second child.

MY EXPERIENCE REVEALED

Of course the best way to learn is to experience the process, so several years ago I decided I wanted to investigate something from my own life. From the age of twelve I had always been adamant that I would never get married or have children, and used to voice these opinions with great conviction.

So not surprisingly I found myself at the age of thirty-seven without a partner; not unhappy, but feeling that something wasn't right and that there was an emotional blockage for me somewhere in my history.

I used the exact same process outlined in this book, and held the intention that if there was a past life connected with my aversion to being married, I wanted to see it and clear it once and for all. My intention was clear and strong, and what I saw was profound and amazing.

I found myself in the deep south of America; it was the mid-1800s, not long before the American Civil War. I was a dark-haired southern belle from a very wealthy family.

My life was unusual in the sense that I was very well educated. My father was a man ahead of his time and saw no reason why his daughter should not be as well educated as his sons. I expressed a strong desire to study and perhaps even pursue a career in the law, as I was passionate about civil rights and social equality. My parents took all of this in their stride and they supported me in most of my endeavours.

At the age of nineteen or twenty I met a man who would succeed in convincing me to marry him. Not only was he charming, handsome, and from a good family, he was also an abolitionist who fought openly for the emancipation of African slaves and better living standards for the large numbers of poor people in our community. After nearly two years of fervent proposals, he managed to convince me I could still have all the freedom I wanted and pursue my interests as his wife. He made it clear that he would encourage and be proud of me, and promised that we could work together. I married him and believed I would be happy.

What I hadn't given much thought to before marrying him was the effect that having children would have on my life. I became pregnant in our first year together and another four children followed in quick succession. The hormonal highs and lows of five pregnancies in five years caused all the other hopes and dreams I had for my life to be thrown to the wind.

I was exhausted and often depressed, plus other problems were brewing on the horizon as well. My husband was becoming increasingly unpopular amongst his wealthy friends and business associates for his unorthodox views and outspoken manner. He was making enemies, his family had all but disowned him, and our financial situation began to deteriorate rapidly.

One night, when my husband was out at a town meeting, I heard shouting and noises coming towards our house. Our home was pretty grand by normal standards, with a long gravel driveway coming up through the garden to the front of the house.

My children and I converged on the front veranda to see men with torches aflame, staggering, hollering, and dragging something behind them. I began to shake, knowing something terrible had happened. I clutched onto my children as one of the men finally came forward from the mob. He announced that my husband had finally "got what he deserved" for supporting black people and making a mockery of everything wealthy, white society had created and stood for.

This dreadful man yelled in this way for a minute or so and then beckoned to some others behind him. My husband's broken and battered body was dragged forward by these men and dumped right in front of us. He was dead; murdered by an angry mob of men who had felt threatened by him.

In that moment, my life was completely destroyed. I was now a widow with five children to support, and no real income. I was distraught, frightened, and instantly broke.

It became clear to me as to why in this life I had been so adamant from a young age never to marry or have children.

With my Angel's help, I sent this life to the Light and let all the pain from that experience go. As always, the positive qualities I had, in addition my positive memories and traits were all returned to me and reintegrated. It was a very powerful and enlightening process. Three weeks later, I met a man whom I married after a year, and there is no doubt in my mind that the understanding and resolution I gained from reviewing and releasing that past life cleared the way for this next important step in my life.

Over the years, I have seen many people experience dramatic changes within themselves and their lives after having a past-life reading with me or from doing the process for themselves.

Physical ailments have dramatically improved, relationships turned around, and deep emotional and psychological traumas have been healed; so much so that I could write a book on these cases alone! Many of the people who come to me do so because they feel lost, confused, directionless, or depressed. Helping them relieve themselves of emotional baggage that had been with them for lifetimes gave them a fresh outlook and renewed energy to embrace life.

One of the most rewarding outcomes is that when we have finished dredging through the difficult and unpleasant stuff we begin to encounter past lives that involved much more happiness, success, and positive memories. Once the shadows are gone from the cupboard, all the positives can be reintegrated as well.

CHAPTER TEN

Healing Self-Sabotage— Your Personality Aspects

When you think about it, you are not just one type of person. You will have many different facets or aspects to your personality that come into play in various situations.

For instance, very few people are extroverted or organised all the time; most of us have days when we feel more introverted and require some solitude, or have one area of our lives which is confused or even chaotic.

Most humans are actually quite paradoxical creatures, full of inconsistencies and contradictions. To me complexity is preferable, as I have never wanted to be squished into one pigeonhole; but for some reason there seems to be a belief floating around our culture that you have to be able to define yourself and who you are in one sentence. Human beings are not one-dimensional. We are wonderfully complex and rich.

Included in the melange of who we are exists the parts of ourselves we like and want everyone else to see, such as the efficient, positive, and successful. However we also have the parts of ourselves we have labelled weak, unlovable, or unworthy, tucked away in the deep drawers and unused cupboards of our complex inner world.

No matter how cleverly you have buried or disguised these negative aspects, they will have an effect on your life, often without you consciously realising it. In fact, I have observed that the aspects most strenuously ignored or denied are the ones that have the most power. It was a wise person who once observed "What you resist, persists."

In this chapter you are going to discover how to stop resisting those parts of yourself you consider unacceptable. Once you do, you'll find that these inner sabotage monsters will transform and start working *for* and *with* you rather than *against* you.

Not long ago, a woman in her forties came to see me for the first time. She had been divorced for about a year, had three children under ten years old living with her, and her ex-husband was, to say the least, not pulling his weight. I did not know any of this when we first met. She had smiled at me sweetly when she came into my room and was very polite as she detailed for me some of her worries and woes.

It was not so much what she was saying that interested me though, because I was becoming increasingly fascinated by the show that was going on in her eyes. There was so much anger in them—with my clairvoyant sight, I could see flames and sharp knives jumping out of her pupils! They weren't directed at me personally; there was so much anger in her system that her Anger Aspect had created this outlet for its self expression.

My Angels kept saying to me "Ask her what she is so angry about," so I did—it was like the whole room shook! She actually braced herself by grabbing the couch with both hands. Then she said "You weren't supposed to see that. I thought I had that all very well hidden." She was amazed that it was so obvious to me, as we had been together for no more than five minutes.

My consultations only last for one hour, so there was no time to waste. We introduced her to her Anger Aspect and it was a pretty wild ride. This aspect, which she believed was so neatly tucked away, began tearing the place apart. On my Inner Screen, I could see it smashing the furniture into twigs, screaming, yelling, and pounding its fists upon the floor. The tirade of angry words that it spoke through me was also very revealing, because much of its anger was directed not just at her ex-husband, but at men in general; particularly her father who had walked out on the family when she was twelve, never to be seen again.

My client's Anger Aspect spat abuse at all men, whom it regarded as irresponsible and worthless. This aspect was also angry at my client for getting married and setting herself up for what it believed was her inevitable disappointment and suffering. It is fortunate that our personality aspects remain nonphysical, because they can certainly be very intense and powerful when they emerge, although that's not to say they don't show up in our physical lives. In this woman's case, for instance, she had a knack for attracting angry behaviour from other people, whether from a complete stranger in another car, or the people she worked with.

In the last year, she had fallen out with friends, been the victim of numerous episodes of road rage, and had to be moved to another department in her company because of the bad vibes between her and some of her colleagues. She'd suppressed anger prior to her divorce, but since the divorce it had multiplied tenfold and was acting like an irresistible magnet for people who wanted to vent their own anger.

The relief from her Anger Aspect came fairly swiftly after the session because she did her homework and observed this aspect regularly until it transformed. She was ashamed of her angry feelings and had hoped she could hide them as we all do with the things we don't like about ourselves. It takes courage to begin to understand the energies at play in your personality. When you do, it can be incredibly liberating.

The woman was greatly relieved to finally have these feelings out in the open as we watched and listened to the fury that poured out of her angry self. Her Angels explained to her that there was no need to feel ashamed or believe she was a bad, angry person. They told her these personality aspects are created when we're very young and unable to deal with painful or frightening situations.

In my client's case, her father's departure had been the last straw in an unhappy relationship with him. The anger she had felt as a little girl about the way he treated her, her mother and siblings, was painful and impossible to rationalise. She knew her father wouldn't listen to her, so apart from the occasional outburst she began to bottle all of those feelings up.

As I have heard the Angels explain many times, the Anger Aspect was formed by her subconscious mind as a survival mechanism. Each Aspect acts as a storage space for various emotions until the individual is mature and strong enough to deal with them at a conscious level.

Very interesting things can start to happen when you own and heal your negative aspects. In this case a man in my client's office asked her out on a date a few months after her first treatment, and his comments were very telling.

When she asked him why he had waited to ask her out, he told her that she'd always seemed a bit prickly and unapproachable, but now there was something a little softer and more open about her. He had picked up on her anger towards men even though he wouldn't have labelled it that way, and he had been afraid she would snap at him.

She began to understand how all the anger that she had suppressed since her childhood had helped set her up for a series of relationships with uncaring men, and then ultimately no relationship at all.

People often say to me that they can now see that a particular aspect has been trying to get their attention for years by creating certain situations over and over again. We attract to ourselves what we carry inside; no amount of frozen smiles or political correctness can fool the Universe.

Percentage-wise, my client's angry self was perhaps only one percent of who she was, but such aspects are very powerful and can end up running our lives if we don't pay attention to their messages.

So how can you get some clues as to what aspects in *you* need healing? Start by looking at what you attract into your life on a daily basis: things that you don't like are not the Universe's way of punishing you, they're red flags being waved from a part of you that needs your help.

Each personality aspect is like a coin, because it has two sides. The positive or flip side of the Anger Aspect is passion (including sexual passion), feistiness, and an ability to stand up for yourself in appropriate ways— all pretty useful qualities, wouldn't you agree? However you can't bury one side of the coin without burying the other, so when you suppress your anger you also suppress your capacity for living your life with passion; when you suppress hatred you suppress your capacity to feel love; when you suppress resentment you suppress your wellspring of forgiveness, and emotional deadness is the result.

When given the right kind of attention, your negative aspects will automatically transform into their positive versions. The process is a matter of degree, as very few people feel complete hatred and no love, but whatever hatred there is can be transformed back into love so their capacity to give, receive, and feel love becomes greater. That makes this one of the most uplifting techniques that I have been given the privilege to work with, because it clearly illustrates that even the darkest parts of us want to make their way back to the Light.

Here is a brief list of some of the negative personality aspects we have come across and their positive transformations:

Negative	Positive
Anger	Passion, feistiness, ability to stand up for oneself
Hatred, self-hatred	Love, self-love
Resentment	Forgiveness
Self-loathing	Self-acceptance
Self-sabotage	Personal empowerment, success, ability to receive good things in life
Poverty, lack, and struggle	Abundance, trusting the flow of life
Pessimism	Optimism
Self-criticism	Confidence
Grief	Joy, happiness
Persecution, feeling picked on or hard done by	Harmony, sense of belonging
Greed	Gratitude and generosity
Fear	Trust and inner strength, feeling safe in the world
Sadness and depression	Happiness and inner peace
Abandonment, outsider, misfit	Knowing you belong, greater ability to connect with others
Self-victimization, blaming	Responsibility for one's decisions and choices
Unappreciation	Self-appreciation

Superiority	Understanding, approachability, empathy
Jealousy, envy, possessiveness	Trust, gratefulness, abundance, generosity, feeling safe
Judgement, excessive criticism	Nonjudgement, acceptance, live-and-let-live attitude
The wounded child	The sensitive child
Shame, loathing of life/self	Self-love, self acceptance, inner peace

So can you now begin to grasp what amazingly multi-faceted beings we are? The list is endless, and the combinations and degrees of expression of each aspect are unique to each person. Naturally we are all endowed with any number of positive aspects such as generosity, kindness, empathy, compassion, curiosity, playfulness, wisdom, creativity, and inventiveness. All these aspects are in each of us, it just depends on which side of the coin is more active, as the extent to which people are stingy is also the extent to which they could become generous, or the extent to which they fear emotional commitment is also the extent to which they long for it.

Working with your own personality aspects will help you unravel your own frustrating complexities and help you express the highest versions of who you are in this life.

There is no limit to the number of aspects you can work with; the list in this book is just a sample of what I've come across. You will also discover as you work your own, so be prepared to go with the flow as that wonderful imagination of yours helps you connect with what's going on inside you.

The number of observation sessions required to transform an aspect is unique to each person, so try not to put limits on your inner work. Sometimes you will be pleasantly surprised at how quickly one evaporates, whilst others will be much more tenacious. Count your blessings—they're showing up and more and more of your own personal energy is transforming into Light. Others will notice the difference in you, and you will certainly notice the positive changes in yourself and the quality of your life.

The Transformation Process

As is the case with all the techniques that my Angels and Spirit Guides have taught me over the years, this one is quite simple. It will be new and unusual to you at first, but that doesn't mean it's difficult to do. My Angels and I have taught hundreds of people how to do this over the years, and everyone has benefited from it.

In this process it is very important to let your imagination flow and give it free rein, as it will be translating your suppressed emotions into images and words for you to experience. The foundation of this process is observation; when you relax, close your eyes, and focus on your Inner Screen, you will be able to observe one of your aspects as though you were watching it on television.

It is important to understand that the simple act of observing whatever negative part of yourself emerges will allow it to heal. Consider that it has been denied and hidden away for almost all your life, expressed only through stress and the occasional outburst. The act of observance means something is no longer hidden or ignored, but acknowledged (in this case) with compassion. That compassion allows a negative aspect to be released and transformed into its positive manifestation.

The Angels advise us that we must always observe wounded aspects of ourselves with detached compassion, acknowledging their presence without judgement. To think of it another way, the negative aspect of yourself is finally getting the chance to reveal itself and come to you for help. You don't have to *do* anything other than observe, meaning that you listen to, watch, and feel this part of you as it expresses itself without hindrance.

Observation here means to have a sense of, be aware of, and let play out whatever's inside you without trying to interfere, censor, or change it. The true meaning of observation in this case is full attention with detached compassion.

Let's also define the meaning of the word "detached" in this situation, because some people mistakenly assume it's something like being aloof. Detachment isn't the same as not caring; it's about respecting the way this part of you needs to express itself, giving it permission to rant, rave, swear, cry, accuse, or whatever it needs to do without trying to change it. Put detachment and compassion together and what you have is acceptance and understanding. All these parts of you need your acceptance, understanding, and of course your attention in order to heal.

OBSERVING NEGATIVE PERSONALITY ASPECTS

Requirements: A quiet space where you can lie or sit comfortably

Time required: 15–30 minutes

- Sit or lie down somewhere you can feel comfortable and relaxed.
- Focus on an area or an issue in your life which regularly causes you problems. It may be that you are always broke, that your relationships never last very long, or that you are always having conflicts with a certain person or type of person. Think more about the actual situation rather than trying to figure out which personality aspect you should be look-

ing at. Everyone is different, there is no formula I can give you, only your Higher Self or subconscious wisdom will know which aspect you need to see most at this time. It may even be more than one, so be open to whatever comes. Note: You cannot force an aspect to reveal itself. By focusing on the actual problem, you create an opening for whatever aspect(s) will show up.

- Set your intention to observe one of these aspects of yourself with detached compassion. Be clear with the intention to not judge, analyse, or try to change it in any way. The Universe takes care of the healing—all you have to do is give your attention.

- The next step is to make your connection to your Guidance through your Channel, so allow yourself a minute or two to feel the light and energy coming down from the Cosmos and up from the Earth.

- Focus on your Inner Screen and ask your Angels and Spirit Guides to help you see the aspect that is ready to reveal itself, and just remain relaxed and attentive. Note: On your first attempt it may take a few minutes before you get a sense of anything. Don't be impatient. These parts of your personality are accustomed to feeling unwanted and hiding themselves away; give them a chance to adjust to the idea that you are now ready to acknowledge them.

- Gradually, you will get a sense of some figure or character emerging. If your clairvoyant sight isn't very clear yet, it can be like a feeling that someone has arrived. You know, a bit like when you know that someone has come into the room without even having to look around; you simply feel a presence.

- Stay as relaxed and focused as you can, continuing to breathe deeply and remain aware of your intention. You will receive some impressions; let your aspect express itself in any way it likes. It cannot actually touch or harm you, no matter how strong its energy.

- Enjoy your observation time, look for all the detail you can, tune in to how you are feeling within yourself—do you suddenly feel angry or sad? Listen attentively as though someone is about to say something very important, and just let the information come. The sad, depressed, and victimised ones may be nothing more than a sobbing heap on the floor.

Your imagination will find some amazing ways to translate the energy of your suppressed emotions to you, like characters from the high dramas of your life. The Anxious Aspect might be in a small room, pacing the floor; a Fear Aspect might be hiding behind a door; a Lonely Aspect may look like an ageing cowboy trudging through the desert on its own; a Judgemental Aspect may be seated behind a huge desk banging a gavel.

How long the observation process goes on for is up to you or your aspect. The aspect may suddenly fade away to indicate that today's viewing is over; another way to know when to stop is when the aspect starts to repeat the same information over and over. The only thing that each aspect knows is the emotion from which it has been created.

Aspects are one-dimensional—they cannot relate to or express anything else—so eventually you'll be watching the same footage in a loop because the aspect will have nothing else to say.

Ultimately, your own ability to stay attentive and focused is most important. If you are tired or concerned about running out of time, you can stop whenever you like. Simply ask your Angels and/or Spirit Guides to come and take over for you, and they will come and surround that aspect in a cocoon of protective white light, taking care of your aspect until you are ready to observe it the next time.

Every observation session will transform that aspect to some degree. Again there is no formula, but generally speaking, one of two things will happen. Each time you go in and observe, you will notice a slight alteration to your aspect.

Let's use a Depressed Aspect as an example. It may start off very morose and negative, looking heavy and dark; but each time you go in and observe it, there is an increasing lightness about it and the negative monologue is not so intense. Eventually, from session to session you actually witness the stages of the transformation process, until all you are shown when you ask to observe your Depressed Aspect is the happy and joyous aspect of yourself.

The other method that has been taught to us is that the negative aspect will simply fade away more with each observation until eventually there is nothing to observe when you call up the Depressed Aspect. It's as though the movie has ended and there's nothing more to show.

Either way, you will know your aspect is healed because you will see the transformed version or your screen will simply be blank. And of course, something else will be different too; you will feel much better within yourself, and attract more positive people and situations into your life because the energy you are giving out is a lot brighter.

It is important to note that healing a Depressed Aspect, for instance, does not mean you can't get depressed again. What you have healed is the baggage you've been carrying around for so long, clearing out the old store to give yourself a fresh start. You will always be capable of feeling any of the negative emotions associated with the negative aspects; having access to the full range of emotions is part of being human.

People often say to me, "I want to get rid of my grief" or "I want to get rid of my anger" as though it's a bad tooth I could just pull out. Emotions aren't like that; the "bad" ones can't just be removed. They are there as a very important part of your intuitive guidance system that helps you to know when you are doing something right for you or not. If you want to be on your highest or most spiritual path in this life, learn to listen to your feelings and emotions. One of the ways we learn about our positive emotions is by experiencing their opposites as well.

Feelings of anger can be a signal that you are in a situation that is unhealthy in some way. Feelings of sadness can indicate that you are suppressing your lifelong dreams and not following your heart, just as sure as the intense sensation of heat can indicate you are about to get burnt! So don't wish your negative emotions away—they are not bad in and of themselves; they only become negative when they are so suppressed that they covertly begin to run your life.

A NEGATIVE PERSONALITY ASPECT REVEALED

"I just can't find anyone I like…"

This was the lament of a man in his late twenties who had been seeing me for some time. He was shy, soft spoken, and even quite withdrawn. After having gotten to know him a little, it didn't surprise me that he didn't socialise much.

I just assumed it was because he needed to work on his confidence. So we began the session and very quickly an aspect of his emerged that took me by surprise. It was his Arrogant Aspect, and it was in full flight.

For the next twenty minutes it spoke through me about all the things it didn't like about the people my client knew. According to this aspect, everyone was inferior to him in some way and not worth the effort or time it took to develop or maintain a friendship.

This Arrogant Aspect also spoke of how it refused to demean itself by doing work it didn't want to do, or even to submit to the kind of questioning most of us consider normal in an interview. Its attitude was "I am better than you and I don't have to prove it. If you can't see how superior I am, that's your problem."

The image I was given of this aspect was of a tall, haughty, middle-aged male, like someone I would expect to see in the British Civil Service or a member of the aristocracy. He even spoke with a formal tone that was nothing like my client's normal voice. My client and I even started to giggle at some of the things the aspect said, they were so snobbish and absurd.

To his credit, my client completely owned the fact that he had always felt that way about other people on some level. Yes, he was genuinely shy and had some issues with feelings of inferiority as well, but he confessed that he knew his arrogance had been there all along and he had often thought of himself as arrogant.

He also admitted that this was indeed one of the reasons that he had not had a job in over a year, preferring to live on the money he made from playing the stock market.

He went home and continued the transformation of his Arrogant Aspect with his own observation sessions, and after a few weeks this aspect did not show up any more, but a new aspect did. The aspect of fear.

Healing his Arrogant Aspect had paved the way for his Fear Aspect to reveal itself; specifically his fear of people.

When the new aspect showed itself my client asked his Angels what kind of aspect it was. They told him it was fear, which correlated with the feelings he had when the new aspect first appeared. He went to work observing this aspect, which gradually resulted in some very deep healing.

He is thirty now, and finally feels strong enough to work and live in a place of his own, knowing he has the tools for self-awareness and healing within him at all times.

CHAPTER ELEVEN

Creating Heart and Mind Balance

These days most of us live in our heads without even realising it. We are often unaware of the stresses we put our bodies through—a lack of exercise or excessive intake of stimulants such as coffee or alcohol can have devastating effects over time.

Often we are even more unaware of our true feelings about many of the most important matters in our lives. Or if we are aware of our feelings, expressing them clearly to others may still be difficult.

In the chapter on Psychic Conversations you learned how to use a tool that can help you to communicate messages that might well be sensitive or volatile in nature. In this chapter you will learn a technique that will help you to express your truth from another level of your being: the level of your heart.

Feeling blocked or embarrassed when it comes to expressing your gentleness and love can create just as many problems in this life as not being able to express your hurt or anger. The Heart-Mind balance will help you to express your heartfelt feelings more comfortably and calm your mind, so that the kind of fear that we justify by labelling it logical or rational will no longer dominate your life.

Once again, the Heart-Mind balance is a technique that was taught to me by my Angels and Spirit Guides while I was working on a client. Since that time, it has been useful in many people's treatments and has become one of the techniques I teach in my courses.

It is such a simple process, easy to do for yourself or another, and its benefits are numerous. If you are very worried about something, have problems with feelings of anxiety, have trouble making decisions, or lack confidence in your decisions, then you can benefit from this technique.

Your heart always knows what to do even when your mind is confused. The Heart-Mind balance strengthens the heart while calming the mind, helping you to feel clearer and more connected to your truth.

Obviously we are not talking about the physical heart which pumps blood through your body. We are talking about that profound part of you represented by the heart chakra, the part of you that feels and expresses love. Look around you now to witness the effects that too much living from the mind has had on our world; conflict, complicated bureaucracies, and an overemphasis on material wealth and being "in control."

Take a moment now to imagine a world where more people lived consistently from their hearts, expressing their love and appreciation, being more receptive emotionally and more aware of the feelings of others.

If global change seems a little ambitious to you, think again, because all great change begins with the individual. When your heart energy is strong, clear, and flowing through your life, you will influence many other people in positive ways and will create a more harmonious life for yourself.

When performing a Heart-Mind balance you should sense a continuous flow of energy between the heart, throat, and brow chakras. The energy flow forms an upright infinity symbol or figure eight, with the throat chakra in the middle serving as the point where the eight crosses over itself.

There is a very good reason why the flow of energy crosses over at the throat forming the figure eight pattern: the throat chakra is at the crossroads of the heart and the mind, dealing with a double dose of energy and often being the central point in a "tug of war" of sorts.

As you clean up the energy which flows around the Heart-Mind configuration, the throat chakra receives a much needed double dose of healing, as it is often very stressed or tense from years of domination by the mind energies and suppression of emotions and feelings. We place a great deal of importance on verbal communication, so our throat chakras are usually required to work very hard in order to help us get the things we say "right" rather than expressing the truth or our true feelings. The following exercise will help you express your truth more clearly and straight from your heart.

As with all techniques in this book, you may do whatever you like to set the scene and help yourself feel more confident and comfortable. If you have any favourite crystals that you would like to place nearby, please do so. Light a candle, put on soft music, or burn some aromatherapy oils or incense. You could also ask your Angels and Spirit Guides to gather closely around you before you begin if it helps you feel more confident. It's your space, so make it all as pleasant as you like, and/or ask the person you're working with what would be most beneficial for him or her.

Exercise Fourteen

Creating Your Own Heart-Mind Balance

Requirements: A quiet location where you can lie or sit comfortably

Time required: 15–30 minutes

- Sit or lie quietly, close your eyes, breathe deeply, relax yourself, and prepare for your visualisation. Set a clear intention to give yourself a lovely Heart-Mind balance.

- Take a moment to remember your connection to your Divine Guidance via your Channel. Spend a minute or two getting yourself connected to the white light coming down through you from the Cosmos, and the warm, red light coming up to you from the core of the Earth.

- Imagine your Angels or Spirit Guides gathering around to support you.

- Now that you have engaged your antenna, take your attention to your Inner Screen as well, remembering that you have this place in your mind where images can be shown to you.

- Focus on your brow, throat, and heart chakras. Imagine a figure eight connecting the three of them with the throat chakra in the centre at the point where the figure eight crosses over.

- Trace this figure eight over your own chakras with your fingertips if you like, to get a feel for where it sits, coming up from your heart, crossing over at the throat, looping up and around through the brow, and then back down through the throat again in the other direction, returning to the heart and so on, in a continuous flow. Note: This is the energy pattern you will be working with to create more balance between your heart and mind. Just like blood is constantly circulating through your arteries and veins, this energy is constantly flowing through this circuit that connects these three chakras.

- Relax, close your eyes and tune in to this energy flow. Imagine it on your Inner Screen if you like and see if you can get a sense of the colour and/or quality of the energy and the three chakras involved. Does the energy flow smoothly, or in fits and starts? How do the chakras feel—is one more blocked, heavy, or tired than the others?

- Often the colour and quality of this energy is greyish, murky, and sluggish. The brow chakra may feel overcharged and busy, and the heart chakra may feel dull, weak, heavy, or even numb. What you are aiming for is a smooth, steady energy flow that feels calm and strong, with no heaviness or blockages in any area; and a nice clean, bright colour to the energy rather than a dull or murky one.

- Once you are at the point where you have a little bit of a feeling for what is happening in your "figure eight" and the three associated chakras, you can call in the healing energy and light to clear and balance it.

- Imagine a beautiful, strong beam of violet light, or whatever colour feels best, flowing down to you from the Cosmos and into your heart chakra at the centre of your chest. Let it keep flowing from the heart chakra into the figure eight until you feel that it has calmed, unblocked, and brightened your energy flow. Imagine it soothing your mind, clearing your throat, and strengthening your heart until your entire system feels refreshed and glowing.

- Finish the exercise by surrounding yourself in a protective cocoon of silver or white light, taking a moment or two to enjoy the feeling of this healthy energy flow. Breathe deeply and become aware of your physical body again. Open your eyes.

TREATING SOMEONE ELSE

Once you have a feel for the Heart-Mind balance and have an understanding of how it works for you, it is quite a simple technique to perform on someone else. Ask their permission first, explain to them what it's about, or have them read this chapter.

Even children as young as five or six will get the gist of what you're offering to do for them if you take the time to explain it in simple terms; you've read the instructions and it really is no more complicated than that. Focus on your intention, which in this case is to give someone you care about a Heart-Mind balance.

Let go of your own opinions on the other person's emotional state or problems. Make it your intention to be the best and clearest Channel for the healing energy you can be. Remember that giving someone a treatment like this is not about you fixing them, but rather helping them gain the clarity and strength to help themselves.

Exercise Fifteen

Treating Someone Else to a Heart-Mind Balance

Requirements: A quiet location where your subject can sit or lie comfortably, but easily accessible to you

Time required: 10–20 minutes

- Have the person lie down and close their eyes. Make sure you can sit or stand comfortably close by.
- Ask your Angels and Spirit Guides to gather around and support you.
- Take a moment to feel your own connection to the Cosmos and the Earth through your Channel.
- On your own body, place your fingertips gently on any two of the three chakras involved in this technique—the heart, throat, and brow—and imagine the cleansing violet light flowing down from the Cosmos, through your Channel and into your heart chakra.
- From there, the light branches off to flow out through both your arms, passing through your shoulders, upper arms, elbows, forearms, and wrists, and finally out through your fingertips and into the person you are working on.
- You are now a Channel or conduit for the energy and light; you don't have to do anything else except keep the flow going by continuing the figure eight

through the three chakras. As human beings, our job is not to be the actual healer, but to strive to be the clearest possible vehicle for the healing energies the Universe naturally provides.

- Move your hands between the three chakras as you feel guided to do so. Check in with your Inner Screen for any vision that might show up.

- Allow the healing energy to flow to and through you into the person's chakras. If you can feel the spin of the chakras or the flow of the energy through your arms and hands or around the person's "figure eight", terrific! If you can't, don't worry. As long as your intention is clear, the Universe will take care of the rest.

- Look for the flow of energy through the figure eight and see if you can notice it clear and change. Feel free to tell the person you're working on what's happening as you work, or wait until you've finished and exchange feedback: whatever feels more comfortable for you.

- Ten or fifteen minutes will be quite enough. When you are ready to finish, imagine yourself wrapping the person in a lovely, soft cocoon of white energy and light and take your hands away.

- Picture yourself standing under a waterfall of silver light that rinses away any energy that you may have absorbed into your field.

- Encourage the person to lie or sit quietly for a minute or two before getting up.

- Make sure that you ask the person you treated to give you some feedback on his or her experiences so you can learn. You might be thrilled to hear reports of feeling warmed and soothed by the energy flowing from your hands.

A HEART-MIND BALANCE RESTORED
She couldn't say "I love you"

Not long after the Angels first taught me this technique, a woman in her thirties came to see me in a state of considerable despair. She had been in a relationship with a man for around three years and had been very happy. Around a year before she came to see me, the woman's boyfriend had began telling her he loved her, and although he was disappointed she didn't say those words back to him, he figured it was only a matter of time. He could feel that she loved him even though she never used those words.

Unfortunately, her inability to say "I love you" had started to become a problem. Her partner began to get angry and feel insecure, accusing her of deliberately withholding or simply not loving him back at all.

In a flurry of tears, my client blurted all this information out in a couple of minutes. She was afraid of admitting her feelings lest she be hurt again, like she had been in the past. My Angels very clearly told me that she needed a Heart-Mind balance, so I did what I was told and worked on her for about a half hour.

As the treatment proceeded, she became so calm and peaceful, her eyes closed and she didn't realise that a gentle smile was beginning to form on her face. It wasn't necessary for me to say anything—I just let the wonderful energy and light do its work.

The woman's heart energy was so constricted, I felt compelled to keep one of my hands on her heart chakra. My other hand moved back and forth between her brow and throat. Slowly, the murky energy that moved sluggishly through her figure eight became brighter and more vibrant; eventually achieving a lovely bluish/violet hue.

When all felt clear and balanced, we wrapped her in a cocoon of light and sent her on her way with a happy expression where a very tense one had been only an hour ago.

A week later she contacted me to tell me that her boyfriend had proposed! She had found the courage to say those magical three words; which was all he had really been waiting for. Feeling more connected to her now than he ever had before, he decided to pop the question and they were both delighted—as was I for them.

Most of us are waiting around for big, earth-shattering miracles to come along and dramatically transform our lives. When we think in such hyperbolic terms, we can easily ignore the fact that smaller miracles are happening for us every day. As you learn to work with the techniques in this book, particularly the ones that most appeal to you, it will become apparent that the ability to effect some of these small miracles is in the palm of your hands. You have nothing to lose and much to gain. Practice, experiment, trust your inner guidance, and enjoy.

Chapter Twelve

Do I Have to Meditate?
No, but it really does help!

You probably weren't expecting a chapter on meditation in a book about developing clairvoyant abilities, but the benefits of meditation are wide ranging, especially in efforts to become more intuitive and clairvoyant.

Most of us lead very busy lives and become all too accustomed to almost unrelenting noise and activity. Constant mental activity often takes the form of planning for the future or worrying about the past, which can create a low-level anxiety that you live with each day and come to believe is normal. Yet it is in the quiet times that your Divine Guidance will reach you most easily. Remember my story about the ringing in my ears at three or four o'clock in the morning?

Many people find their early attempts at meditating dull and frustrating. We're so familiar with constantly thinking or having something going on around us to entertain or distract that inner silence is *very* unfamiliar territory. I know meditating can be difficult at first, but eventually you'll come to wonder how you ever got along without it.

Meditation is a way of quieting the clamour of the mind while resting your body and mind together. As a result of regular meditation many people experience a greater sense of inner calm, improved concentration, more refreshing sleep, and even physical benefits such as the lowering of blood pressure or the improvement of certain illnesses or conditions.

At first, taking the time out to meditate may seem to be a problem for busy people. It may even seem to be a waste of time because nothing appears to be happening. For most of us, any kind of endeavour can only be considered fruitful when it produces something obvious and tangible. But the "nothing happening" part of meditation is really the key, as it gives your mind time to rest and unravel for a while.

Some of the most successful, effective, efficient, and productive people I know meditate regularly. Corporations all around the world are now paying for their top employees to learn how to meditate to ensure calmer attitudes and increased productivity. These companies and their CEOs might not think of these practices as meditation; perhaps they have a catchier and more modern label such as "mind focusing techniques," but it's all meditation no matter how you package it.

If you're an ambitious, goal-oriented person or if you simply want to get more out of your life and create a sanctuary of peace within yourself available to you twenty-four hours a day, I recommend you begin to meditate in some way. Once a day is great, but you will benefit from it even if you only manage occasional practice.

How Do I Meditate?

There is no one "right" way to meditate, but all forms of meditation involve focusing the mind in some way.

One of the greatest obstacles to meditation for many people seems to be the idea that you must sit cross-legged, completely immobile, and in silence and isolation. Quite understandably, this approach is somewhat daunting and unappealing. It simply isn't possible for all of us to behave like yogis or Zen Buddhists; what's important is that meditation becomes an enjoyable practice for you.

There is nothing wrong with meditating when you are seated, curled up on the couch, or stretching out in bed. You can meditate on the bus on your way to work, or while you are working on your tan at the beach. If you close your eyes and breathe deeply for five minutes during your lunch break, that can be a meditation.

Develop a realistic approach that allows your meditation practice to become an integral part of your lifestyle.

Interestingly, there are many additional activities that can be undertaken as meditation. In many cultures, meditation practices include walking, chanting, singing, eating, dancing, and more. If any of these activities gives you pleasure, use them as part of your meditation practice.

Meditation is all about focusing your mind, especially as a beginner. As you're enjoying your walk along the beach or in the park, inhale and exhale deeply. Focus your attention on the rhythm of your footsteps, the patterns in the sand or grass, the sound of the waves or birds, or anything else that absorbs your attention in a gentle and relaxing way.

Eating is the same. How often do you hurry through a meal, finish it, and then don't even really remember enjoying it? Focus on your food—appreciate the beautiful colours, aromas, and textures. Notice all the different flavours that come with every mouthful. Don't take your attention from the food until the meal is finished.

By focusing your mind on a pleasurable activity, noticing the details and sensations in a simple or everyday act, letting the rhythm and energy of life flow through you as you flow with it, you are undertaking a form of meditation.

EXERCISE SIXTEEN

A SIMPLE MEDITATION PRACTICE

Requirements: A quiet, dark, or softly lit place where you
can sit comfortably
Candle
Box of matches

Time required: 10 minutes

- Place your unlit candle in front of where you will sit.
- Seat yourself comfortably in front of the unlit candle. Breathe deeply and take a moment to relax.
- Light your candle, taking time to notice the sparking of the match or the dancing of the flame. Watch the flame as you move it to the candle wick and light it.
- Blow out the match and watch as the smoke drifts away.
- Focus your attention gently on the candle flame; do not stare at it, just let your gaze soften as you watch it.
- Allow your breathing to become deeper and slower.
- Give all your attention to the candle flame for several minutes. As other thoughts enter your mind, let them drift away rather than latching onto them.
- When you achieve a sense of quiet calm and your mind is empty of all thoughts, sit quietly and contemplate the candle flame, noticing how it flickers or how the light is diffused around it.
- When you are ready to finish, take another deep breath, blink your eyes a few times, and blow the candle out. Remain seated for a few moments, enjoying your state of relaxation before resuming your other activities.

Other Meditation Techniques

One of the easiest ways to get into meditation is by listening to a recording of a guided meditation. A guided meditation is just like a story that guides you through a relaxing series of images to help focus your mind in a gentle and flowing way. Listening to this kind of recording gives your mind something to focus on without placing demands on you or forcing you to think.

There are many meditation CDs available today, even in the most mainstream of music and bookstores. Some will have the voice of the facilitator only, some will have music only and most will have both, so make sure you read the description on the packaging first and choose one that focuses on topics or themes you will find helpful.

For example my own meditation CD has five different meditations ranging in length from around nine minutes to sixteen minutes. Each meditation has a different theme, such as helping you to become more aware of the Angels that surround you, or guiding you on a peaceful journey through a beautiful, enchanted forest.

You may also like to try meditating in silence or with your favourite soothing music playing softly, allowing the beauty of the sounds to transport you to a more harmonious inner state.

Instead of trying to empty your mind and "think" about nothing, an easier method is to simply focus your mind on a peaceful theme or image. Use your imagination to help you feel like you are floating in the clouds or sitting on a mountainside surrounded by flowers and endless natural beauty. Whatever appeals to you in the moment is fine. If other thoughts intrude, gently let them go and return to your pleasant meditations.

Another useful technique is to repeat a word or short phrase over and over in you mind, rolling it over in your thoughts like a pebble in a stream. It may be a word with a lot of meaning, such as "love," "joy," or "peace"; or a phrase with great healing power such as "I forgive myself" or "I love myself." Repetition will help to keep your mind from wandering in other directions.

When meditating in complete silence, just let whatever thoughts or memories that surface come up and float away. Rather than getting drawn into one train of thought, allow your thoughts to float through your mind; imagine them evaporating or being blown away like small clouds on a summer breeze.

Meditating in silence can be amazing: it gives you a glimpse of all the memories and feelings you've stored away within yourself throughout your life and may give you some clues as to which Aspects you may need to observe, or insights into some of your past lives.

It can also be a wonderful time for ideas and inspiration. Keep your pen and notebook near you if you like, so when you are finished you can jot down any helpful or creative ideas that may have come to you during the meditation. The power of silence creates the space for you to receive brilliant ideas, solutions to problems, and prompts about important things because when the chatter of your mind slows down, your Angels, Spirit Guides, and Divine Guidance are much more easily heard.

It is also beneficial during meditation to focus your attention on your breathing. Keeping your breath deep and rhythmic is one of the most effective ways to soothe yourself and remove your attention from the mind. Picture the air entering your body and flowing deep into your lungs. Feel its life-giving energy going into every cell.

If you have a sore, stiff, or tense muscle or joint, or general pain somewhere, imagine your breath flowing to and through this area of your body and releasing that pain or discomfort.

The in-breath brings in healing light and energy and the out-breath takes the pain, tension, or blockage away. At the very least, being more aware of your breathing will help to supply more oxygen to your body, warm you up, aid circulation, and encourage you to breathe more fully throughout your life. Shallow breathing is just one of the unfortunate side effects of a stressful lifestyle, so breathe deeply while you meditate to reap the healing benefits.

Closing your eyes while meditating is preferable, as it encourages you to focus your attention inward and connects you with your inner world. It is also more relaxing, both for your eyes and your mind. If you prefer to keep your eyes open, make sure your eyelids are soft. Focus on something close by like your hands or something attractive like a candle flame.

How Often Should I Meditate?

Once a day is great if you can manage it, at a time that suits you. If you find it stressful to add another activity to your morning schedule, try meditating at night, as it can also help you have a more restful night's sleep.

Use your common sense and make meditation work for you. If you find that five or ten minutes is your maximum to begin with, that's fine. Eventually you will find that you can extend that time, or treat yourself to a nice long meditation whilst having a luxurious Sunday bath.

Combine meditation with things you already enjoy doing. Be inventive and don't put pressure on yourself to live up to someone else's standards. Plan your meditation times as times that are important for you and a wonderful way to benefit the development of your intuitive and clairvoyant abilities. Enjoy!

CHAPTER THIRTEEN

Our Enlightened Children

Hopefully by now you've had the opportunity to discover some of your own natural intuitive and clairvoyant skills. Try to imagine what your life might have been like if you had known how to use them since you were a child.

Ponder this for a moment, because the differences and the possibilities are truly astounding. Do you think your struggles in life would have been as difficult or lasted as long if you could have cleared and released some of your past lives in your teens?

Would you have felt so alone or frightened during the trying times if you had known how to connect and communicate with your Angels and Spirit Guides?

Is it possible that you might've had a stronger sense of self and your life purpose if you had known how to keep your chakras, Channel, and Inner Screen open and strong?

Would you have been so easily swayed by other people's opinions if you had been able to receive Divine Guidance through automatic writing?

Is it possible that you would love and accept yourself more today if you had known how to heal and transform the negative personality Aspects that caused inner and outer conflict in your life?

Children are naturally intuitive and clairvoyant, and in many ways the children of today are much more advanced in these areas than most adults. If you have children of your own or come into contact with them, you can be supportive of these innate skills even if you don't fully understand them.

When children are born, their physical body is 100 percent here, but they are still very strongly connected to the Light. Their crown chakras (fontanelles) and Channels are very open and strong—it's as though infants exist in two worlds.

As the days and weeks pass, the soul gradually adjusts to the physical body that it has taken on in order to journey through yet another lifetime. At around the age of two to three years the adjustment process can become a little traumatic, as the intensifying focus on the physical life pulls them increasingly away from the previous realm they inhabited.

There is often a kind of rebellion against the relatively restrictive and heavy nature of physical life. The child is now expected to toilet train, eat more solids, feed itself and learn all the other basics of coping with the outside world, with increasingly less time available for the all-important inner world and life.

The next, most noticeable stage of rebellion is usually the teenage years, and this is no coincidence. Since the age of two or three the child has continued to adjust to its new environment, but is generally still protected from many of life's demands thanks to the parents. During the teen years it becomes very obvious to the child that it will soon have to fend for itself, and the increased demands of coping in the physical world takes the child even further away from its spiritual connections.

In the teen years more and more emphasis is placed on study, knowledge, logic, success, accumulation, achievement, competition, career and the future.

The youngest person I have worked with was seven years old. I have found whenever I have the privilege of working with such young ones they easily comprehend the information I channel and my descriptions of what I am doing.

If I describe one of their Angels, tell them about the colours of their chakras, or clear a past life that has come up to be released, they often respond by saying they already knew about it and had seen some of it before.

Parents often tell me about how their child sees clouds of colour around people (the aura), or how their young children "just knew things" without any logical way of having been informed. As adults, we underestimate children all the time; if we cannot understand their natural connection to the other dimensions that surround us we usually relegate it to the realms of imagination and fantasy, as something strange (even inconvenient) and "just a phase."

Teenage rebellion is often dismissed as a lack of understanding about the way things are, and how the real world "works," but what are we defending? I believe we should encourage teens' spiritedness and individuality instead of putting so much energy into forcing them to conform. Who knows, we might even be able to learn something from them!

Of course children need guidelines to help them with the process of growing up, and they benefit from the experience of their parents and other elders. What they don't need is to be stifled by our fears or our ignorance. Encourage your children to talk about the things they see and believe, especially what you may define as "not real." Ask them to describe such things to you in detail. Have the courage to acknowledge that anything is possible.

Help them to understand they have chosen a journey here in the physical realm, so it's important to be on the best possible terms with life here on earth, whilst reassuring them that they can maintain their connections to the unseen or nonphysical realms as well.

Physical life is to be treasured, savoured, and enjoyed. It is a journey that provides the opportunity for enormous spiritual growth, but it is not the only reality we need stay connected to during this lifetime.

Eastern cultures have long since known of the cyclical nature of all life. Concepts such as reincarnation and practices such as meditation are part of that culture's daily life and many things we westerners still think of as weird or too "out there" are ordinary to them.

Talk to your children about having Angels and Spirit Guides around them; explore books on chakras together, especially ones with lovely, colourful pictures. Ask them what they understand about the idea of reincarnation and whether they feel they have lived here before.

More than once I have listened to a shocked client tell me about how their child knew what a certain location would look like, without the child having been there before in this life.

I once gave a small crystal to a child who had sores in her mouth because my Guidance told me that this particular stone would help heal those sores. "Great!" I thought, "She can hold onto the crystal or put it beside her bed—won't that be lovely?" To my surprise, this very aware two-year-old took the crystal from me, and with considerable gravity, explained that the stone would only help her if she held it in her mouth! When her mother and I both looked alarmed she reassured us that she would sit still while it was in her mouth and that she wouldn't swallow it.

Later that week, when her sores had cleared up and she was feeling better, her mother took her to a crystal shop where she confidently chose a selection for herself. The mother was amazed at the connection her child obviously felt with some of the crystals, and at how definite she was about wanting some and not others.

Another girl of around three years of age was delighted when I told her I love to hug trees. I picked her up and we hugged some beautiful ones together. She said she could feel their energy and that some of them spoke to her.

What I'm getting at is that we can learn a lot from our children and younger generations in general. Every person has a unique, special brand of wisdom, regardless of formal education, "spirituality," and age. The young bring with them incredible awareness and understanding which helps our entire species step up to a new level of consciousness.

Whether you call them Rainbow, Crystal, or Indigo Children, it matters not—the wise ones are here, and the sooner we notice the better things will be for everyone.

There is a lovely saying I'm sure many of you already know, and it goes something like this: "We are not human beings having a spiritual experience; we are spiritual beings having a human experience." Our children know this—help them not to forget, while you do your best to understand.

Exercise Seventeen

Learning from Our Children

Requirements: A child (son, daughter, niece, nephew, grandchild, or friend's child) who is happy to chat with you for a while
A quiet place where you and the child can sit and talk

Optional: Paper, colouring pencils, crayons, markers

Time required: 10 minutes—or as long as you like

- Ask the child to tell you what they know about Angels, Faeries, and Invisible or Imaginary Friends.
- Listen to what they say without contradicting or correcting them.
- Explain to your child that you would like to know more about your Guides or Angels and that you would like their help.
- Ask the child what they notice around you, without influencing what might be said. The child may comment about colours, shadows, or people around you; encourage them to expand on any of this without leading.
- If they are willing, ask the child to draw what they are picking up on, using the media provided.
- Once the child has finished telling you or drawing, offer your thanks for the help and let the child know how special and clever they are.

- Treasure the information or pictures you have been given forever.

A Child's Belief Revealed

Although we all know that children have a special connection with their pets, I was reminded how strong and loving a bond that can be when a friend of mine had to take a much-loved family dog to the vet's for a serious operation.

My friend and her husband were very upset and worried, fearing their pet would not survive. They were equally worried about their daughter, who had a strong affection for the dog and would no doubt be devastated by the loss.

I went to speak to their daughter, who was only four years old, hoping to give her a hug and some words of comfort. I managed a few awkward comments before she smiled and put her hand on my arm, to reassure me.

"I'm not worried," she said. "I know he will be all right."

I smiled at her calm face. "How do you know that?" I asked.

"The Angels told me he would be fine," she replied.

She was so bright-eyed, positive, and certain that I knew I didn't have to say anything more to her.

A week later the dog came home from the vet, and just as the Angels had promised, was in great shape. That was several years ago—the dog is still fine!

Be Inspired

About the Author

BelindaGrace has a thriving practice in Sydney and in Ballina, New South Wales, where she sees private clients and also offers telephone readings with clients from all over the world. She regularly conducts courses and workshops around Australia and New Zealand and is the author of a fascinating range of books, CDs, and Oracle cards. BelindaGrace is passionate about helping people discover a deeper meaning and purpose to their lives in order to create a sound foundation of emotional and spiritual health, from which all other areas may thrive.

In her spare time, BelindaGrace loves to enjoy the peace and beauty of her seaside home on the east coast of Australia If you wish to find out more about BelindaGrace and her work, please visit www.belindagrace.com.

SUGGESTIONS FOR
FURTHER READING

Further Reading for Chapter Four

Brennan, Barbara Ann. *Hands of Light: A Guide to Healing Through the Human Energy Field.* New York: Bantam, 1988.

Bruyere, Rosalyn L. *Wheels of Light: Chakras, Auras, and the Healing Energy of the Body.* New York: Fireside Publishing, 1994.

Myss, Caroline. *Anatomy of the Spirit: The Seven Stages of Power and Healing.* New York: Three Rivers Press, 1996.

Further Reading for Chapter Five

Cooper, Diana. *A Little Light on Angels.* Findhorn, Scotland: Findhorn Press, 1998.

Virtue, Doreen. *Angel Therapy: Healing Messages for Every Area of Your Life.* Carlsbad, CA: Hay House Publishing, 1997.

———. *Archangels and Ascended Masters.* Carlsbad, CA: Hay House Publishing, 2004.

Website: www.crystalinks.com—A great resource for all subjects in this book, including Angels and Ascended Masters.

Further Reading for Chapter Six

Murphy, Joseph. *The Power of Your Subconscious Mind.* New York: Bantam, 2001.

Further Reading for Chapter Seven

McCoy, Edain. *How to Do Automatic Writing.* St. Paul, MN: Llewellyn Publications, 2002.

Roman, Sanaya. *Opening to Channel: How to Connect with Your Guide.* Tiburon, CA: HJ Kramer, 1993.

Further Reading for Chapter Eight

Mark, Barbara, and Trudy Griswold. *Angelspeake: How to Talk with Your Angels.* New York: Simon & Schuster, 1995.

Webster, Richard. *Spirit Guides & Angel Guardians: Contact Your Invisible Helpers.* St. Paul, MN: Llewellyn Publications, 1998.

Further Reading for Chapter Nine

Weiss, Brian. *Many Lives, Many Masters.* New York: Fireside, 1988.

Whitton, Joel, and Joe Fisher. *Life Between Life.* New York: Warner Books, 1988.

Further Reading for Chapter Ten

Myss, Caroline. *Sacred Contracts: Awakening Your Divine Potential.* Carlsbad, CA: Hay House Publishing, 2004.

Stone, Hal, and Sidra Winkleman. *Embracing Ourselves: The Voice Dialogue Manual.* Novato, CA: Nataraj Publishing, 1989.

Further Reading for Chapter Twelve
The Venerable Yeshe Chodron. *Everyday Enlightenment: How to Be a Spiritual Warrior at the Kitchen Sink.* New York: HarperCollins, 2006.

Moore, Thomas. *Care of the Soul.* New York: Harper-Collins, 1994.

Further Reading for Chapter Thirteen
Burns, Litany. *The Sixth Sense of Children: Nurturing Your Child's Intuitive Abilities.* New York: Penguin Putnam, 2002.

Twyman, James F. *Emissary of Love: The Psychic Children Speak to the World.* Charlottesville, VA: Hampton Roads Publishing Company, 2002.

Virtue, Doreen. *Indigo, Crystal, and Rainbow Children.* Carlsbad, CA: Hay House Publishing, 2005.

General Recommended Reading
Hawkins, David R. *Power vs. Force: The Hidden Determinants of Human Behavior.* Carlsbad, CA: Hay House Publishing, 2002.

Rasha. *Oneness: The Teachings.* Santa Fe: Earthstar Press, 1998.

Walsch, Neale Donald. *Communion with God*. New York: Berkley Publishing, 2000.

———. *The Complete Conversations with God*. New York: Penguin, 2005.

Yogananda, Paramahansa. *Autobiography of a Yogi*. New York: Crystal Clarity Publishers, 1995. First published 1946 by The Philosophical Library.